PRAISE FOR SPEAK WELL AND PROSPER: TIPS, TOOLS, AND TECHNIQUES FOR BETTER PRESENTATIONS

"If you only have the opportunity to read one book on presentation skills this year, I highly recommend, *Speak Well and Prosper: Tips, Tools, and Techniques for Better Presentations*. You will receive real-life, how-to tips, tools, and solutions to improve every presentation from one-on-one encounters to groups ranging from two to two thousand. Frank has been a public speaker, presentation skills coach, and Toastmaster for over 30 years, and his experience and expertise is evident throughout every page in *Speak Well and Prosper*."

—Arnold Sanow, MBA, CSP (Certified Speaking Professional), Professional Speaker, Trainer, Presentation Skills Coach, and author of 7 books to include *Present with Power, Punch, and Pizzazz . . . The Ultimate Guide to Delivering Presentations with Poise, Persuasion, and Professionalism*

"This is a thoughtful book on the many benefits of speaking well and the discipline and process you need to get there. Frank covers a variety of important communication situations and walks you through how to handle each one with confidence and professionalism from his unique vantagepoint and experience."

—Allison Shapira, Leadership Communication Speaker, Entrepreneur, Founder/CEO of Global Public Speaking, Author of *Speak with Impact: How to Command the Room and Influence Others*

"I have worked with Frank DiBartolomeo for several years now, and I can tell you he poured everything he has into *Speak Well and Prosper: Tips, Tools, and Techniques for Better Presentations*. He took all of his experience and knowledge and packaged it in a way that can truly help you improve your ability to be a better speaker, presenter, and resource to the people you work with and for."

— Mark Levin, CAE, CSP, Leadership and Membership Expert, author of *The Gift of Leadership: How to Relight the Volunteer Spirit in the 21st Century* and *Managing the Membership Experience: Using Membership Mapping to Engage Members and Give Them the Experiences They Want and Value*

"Every successful businessperson knows that public speaking has been an important factor in their climb. In *Speak Well and Prosper: Tips, Tools, and Techniques for Better Presentations*, Frank DiBartolomeo provides a wide-ranging survey of the skills and techniques necessary to acquire and polish this crucial business technique."

— Robert Keiper, Presentation Skills Coach, Author, Speaker, Workshop Leader

"When it's your turn to speak, it always matters, it always requires planning, and it always demands your best effort. *Speak Well and Prosper: Tips, Tools, and Techniques for Better Presentations* will help teach you how to do just that!"

—Rob Jolles, President, Jolles Associates, Inc., thirty-five-year Professional Speaker, and Bestselling author of *How to Change Minds, Why People Don't Believe You, Customer Centered Selling, How to Run Seminars & Workshops*, and *The Way of the Road Warrior*

"Frank DiBartolomeo has nailed it with his book, *Speak Well and Prosper: Tips, Tools, and Techniques for Better Presentations*. He shares valuable insights and actionable suggestions to improve your speaking and presentations. His tips include knowing the importance of being prepared to win; if your fearful of speaking, learn about your audience; and be a "Go-Giver" (give more value than you are paid, increase the # of others you serve, and put others' interests first). I'm using his advice as standard practice when I present and speak!"

—Wendy King, Leadership Expert, and Speaker, Founder of Speakers Without Borders Speakers Bureau, former CFO West Virginia University Health Sciences Center.

"In *Speak Well and Prosper: Tips, Tools, and Techniques for Better Presentations*, Frank DiBartolomeo does a very thorough job of presenting the case for why speaking well is necessary. He wonderfully presents what is only important if you want to advance - in any career! This book is well researched and organized. Each section of the book builds on the section before. It allows the novice presenter to build their speech with the confidence of a clear, easy format to follow and allows the seasoned speaker to become even better at their craft. Frank shares stories that make it an easy and enjoyable read. I am confident you will improve if you just use the information found in this book and continue to practice, practice, practice using the "DiBartolomeo Encyclopedia of How to Speak Well!" An excellent book!!!"

—Dee Taylor-Jolley, Chief Operations Officer, Willie Jolley Worldwide, Chief Learning Officer, The Back Office Boss

"One of the key secrets of business and organizational success has always been the people who communicate and present themselves well, rise to the top. The keys to accomplish this secret are revealed when you read *Speak Well and Prosper: Tips, Tools, and Techniques for Better Presentations*. The strategies are classic, proven and time-tested. You can't afford to be without these modern tools!"

—Shelley Row, PE, CSP, Founder & CEO – Blue Fjord Leaders, Inc. Magazine Top 100 Leadership Speaker | Trainer | Coach | Author of *Think Less, Live More: Lessons from a Recovering Over-Thinker*

"In *Speak Well and Prosper: Tips, Tools, and Techniques for Better Presentations*, Frank DiBartolomeo has lived up to the title. He does provide tips, tools, and techniques that are easily applied to everyday settings in which one uses the spoken voice. No matter where you are in your speaking career, novice or expert, there is something for you! The 'Calls to Action' inspire the reader to do just that—take action—and do it now. There is a sense of urgency in Frank's style that encourages the reader to adopt a 'Can' attitude and just do it. I highly recommend *Speak Well and Prosper*."

—Sharon M. Weinstein, MS, RN, CRNI-R, FACW, FAAN, CSP CEO, SMW Group LLC and Founder, The Global Education Development Institute, Coaching—Consulting—Speaking. We work with companies to enhance retention, empower staff, and enrich the workplace through WOWTcomes™

"There are so many powerful messages in *Speak Well and Prosper: Tips, Tools, and Techniques* by Frank DiBartolomeo. I especially like that Frank included a section on speaking during a crisis and a reminder that "a calm mind generates power." Also his call-to-action at the end of every chapter helps to refine and remind you what the biggest takeaways are. *Speak Well and Prosper* is packed with clear, concise ideas and techniques that can be used immediately. I highly recommend it."

—**Janice Litvin, Workplace Wellness Speaker, Coach and Author of**
Banish Burnout Toolkit

"Now more than ever, how we 'present' makes all the difference for those of us wanting to get our message out there. And, there is nothing like *Speak Well and Prosper: Tips, Tools, and Techniques* to teach us how. Thank you, Frank, for reminding us all how important our authenticity and integrity are to the strength of our voice. What an enjoyable, empowering read!"

—**Madelaine Claire Weiss, LICSW, MBA, BCC, Executive Coach, Speaker, Trainer and Author of the forthcoming book *Getting to G.R.E.A.T:***
5-Step Strategy for Work and Life

"In the foreword Arnold Sanow writes, Zig Ziglar once said, "You can get anything you want in life if you help enough other people get what they want." That is what Frank DiBartolomeo has done in his new book, *Speak Well and Prosper: Tips, Tools, and Techniques for Better Presentations*. He takes you from the 50,000-foot level of speaking to the nitty gritty level. One of my favorite chapters was entitled "Speak Positive – Gain Power". It provides great tips that are particularly important when speaking but also great advice for other parts of our lives as well. In the chapter entitled, "Speak Powerfully with Power Words," he gives wonderful examples of words and phrases that can be used in so many powerful ways. Then he gets technical and gives great advise on technology and speaking virtually. Powerful and invaluable information!"

—**Coni K Meyers, LMC, CLBC, CDC. Leadership Clarity and Crisis Management Strategist, Founder of CKM Solutions Group – Best Selling Author – Speaker – Author of the soon to be released new book, *When the Unthinkable Happens...Be Prepared! Be Ready! helps consumers know what to do to be prepared.* Our "Crisis Knowledge Management Certification" is helping 30 million Americans become better prepared for disasters and crisis.**

"*Speak Well and Prosper: Tips, Tools, and Techniques for Better Presentations* is brilliant and timely. I've always known that Frank

DiBartolomeo is a genius, and this book is one more proof of this fact."

—Mitzi Perdue (Mrs. Frank Perdue), Author with Mark Victor Hansen
of *How to Be Up in Down Times*

"*Speak Well and Prosper: Tips, Tools, and Techniques for Better Presentations* is a comprehensive, motivating, and action-oriented 'How To' guide that will help you greatly improve your presentation content and delivery. It provides an easy-to-follow roadmap to developing consistent, persuasive, and captivating presentations that deliver your intended message. If you ever have an opportunity to influence anyone to your way of thinking, this is the book for you. It's a must read!"

—Carl Savino, President, Corporate Gray and author of *The Military to Civilian Transition Guide*

"Frank and I first met over twenty years ago, when we were teaching Systems Engineering at the Defense Acquisition University. He was an excellent teacher and coach then, but after reading *Speak Well and Prosper: Tips, Tools, and Techniques for Better Presentations*, I realized how Frank has further refined and improved his speaking skills and coaching ability to a world class level. *Speak Well and Prosper: Tips, Tools, and Techniques for Better Presentations* is well researched and serves as an extensive source of practical advice for technical people to improve their speaking skills. It is well written, easy to read, and can greatly accelerate improving your speaking efficiency and effectiveness. I will add Frank's book to my handful of reference books on my desk. You should, too!"

—William Fournier CSEP-Acq., ESEP, CC, LSS GB and Program Management Decision Brief Course Director

"*Speak Well and Prosper: Tips, Tools, and Techniques for Better Presentations* is a must read for anyone wishing to enhance their communication skills. Whether chairing a meeting, giving a presentation or participating in a conference call, this well organized and concisely written book provides timely guidance to maximize your being heard and understood."

—Martin Mahon, Ph.d, Founder and Principal – Xamroc Construction Company, CAPT USN (Ret)

"*Speak Well and Prosper: Tips, Tools, and Techniques for Better Presentations* is a must-have book for anyone who needs to speak, persuade, influence, or communicate. Each chapter provides the reader with Call to Action items to use immediately. Just one idea from this invaluable reference guide can change your life! Get this book and use it NOW!"

> **— Darlene T. Carver, CEO, Merlin & Associates, Inc., National Speakers Association (NSA) Washington DC Chapter Speaker Academy Dean, Presentation Skills Coach, and Contributing Author of *100 Habits from the Happiest Achievers on the Planet***

"Whether you speak to one person or five-hundred, work from the kitchen table or the conference table, *Speak Well and Prosper: Tips, Tools, and Techniques for Better Presentations* is an essential addition to your personal improvement collection!"

> **—Peter Colwell, "Keep At It" Coach, Motivational Speaker, Dale Carnegie Trainer, Author of *Spell SUCCESS in Your Life & Invest in Your Attitude*, www.PeterColwell.com**

"I recommend Frank's new book, *Speak Lead and Prosper: Tips, Tools, and Techniques for Better Presentations* to any leader, speaker or individual who wants to influence others. As a speaker, facilitator and Professional EOS (Entrepreneur Operating System) Implementer with a strong grounding in compelling communications, I value Frank's practical Calls-to-Action and the detailed emphasis on both presentation preparation and delivery. Especially in a virtual world. this book will take you to speaking well and prospering!"

> **—Beth Berman, Professional EOS Implementer, Speaker & Facilitator CEO/Founder Compellications**

"In a career spanning more than 40 years in which I started, led, and restructured a number of companies and business units, I learned early on the importance of effective communication. A specific part of one's success in any field is the ability to communicate in ways that people are engaged in what one has to say and clearly understands the content being shared. Frank DiBartolomeo's book *Speak Well and Prosper: Tips, Tools, and Techniques for Better Presentations* captures the key concepts for effectively communicating in engaging and compelling ways. The strategies and tools contained in this book are essential for anyone who aspires to be successful and to communicate to others in ways that are clearly understood, aspirational and motivational that energize audiences. I highly recommend this book to be part of anyone's tool kit and resource library in order to succeed and reach others."

—**Michael J. Curran, CEO, Curran Advisors, Elevating Leadership, Developing Teams and Building Organizations; co-Author of** *Leadership in Trying Times: Advice to Lead and Succeed*

"Frank DiBartolomeo's book, *Speak Well and Prosper: Tips, Tools, and Techniques for Better Presentations* is a great compilation of no-nonsense tips and strategies to help you connect with your audience for a winning presentation that you can be proud of. Well done!"

— **Cathy Richards, Lifestyle and Wellness Speaker, Inspiring Vitality, author of** *BOOM: 6 Steps to a Longer, Healthier Life*

"Once again, Frank DiBartolomeo has hit the mark. No matter how much you know, if you cannot present that knowledge in a fun and compelling manner you waste yours and the audience's time. Frank knows how to present well and how to help you present well also. Take time to get to know, *Speak Well and Prosper: Tips, Tools, and Techniques for Better Presentations*. I highly recommend Frank's outstanding work."

—**Michael Butera, President and CEO, Association Activision, LLC; Executive Team Coach and Professional Speaker.**

"*Speak Well and Prosper: Tips, Tools, and Techniques for Better Presentations* offers practical suggestions that can be used instantly. It is an enjoyable read with easy-to-follow calls to action throughout the book. For those looking to improve their speaking skills, this is a must read."

—**Lewis Flax, Dale Carnegie Trainer, President Flax Associates**

"Frank DiBartolomeo's book, *Speak Well and Prosper: Tips, Tools, and Techniques for Better Presentations* captures what excellent presentation skills is about for now and into the future. This is must reading for anyone interested in staying or getting ahead of the pack."

— Gerald Edgley, Principal, Jerry Edgley and Associates LLC, Leadership Consultant

"I wish Frank DiBartolomeo's book, *Speak Well and Prosper: Tips, Tools, and Techniques for Better Presentations* existed years ago while I was struggling to deliver engaging, compelling presentations to shareholders. This book provides an excellent roadmap to help develop consistent, compelling presentations that deliver consistent messaging. It reminds us of the importance of engagement with the audience while delivering a message and the importance of entertaining the audience to maintain focus. This book is an excellent tool for developing one's confidence and success as a presenter."

—Paul Perciavalle, former Senior Program Manager, CSRA, Inc.

"*Speak Well and Prosper: Tips, Tools, and Techniques for Better Presentations* is jam packed with real life, how-to information that can be used instantly. At last, a presentation skills book that is practical and not theoretical—written by a presentation skills expert, Frank DiBartolomeo, who knows what he is talking about. This is a practical no-nonsense guide to what really works in delivering a presentation. Read it, internalize it and apply what it says to watch your career soar!"

—Deepak Bhinge, P.E., PMP, CCM

"*Speak Well and Prosper: Tips, Tools, and Techniques for Better Presentations* is a friendly and useful reminder that, when it comes to public speaking, we can all do better. Frank's book provides a very clear and compelling path as to how. Highly recommended for speakers of all experience levels."

—Dan Bozung, author of *This Civilian Sh*t Is Hard: From the Cockpit, Cubicle, and Beyond*

Speak Well and Prosper: Tips, Tools, and
Techniques for Better Presentations

by Frank DiBartolomeo, Jr.

ISBN 978-1-64663-240-4

Published by

◤ köehlerbooks™

3705 Shore Drive
Virginia Beach, VA 23455
800-435-4811
www.koehlerbooks.com

Speak
Well
AND Prosper

Tips, Tools, and
Techniques for
Better
Presentations

Frank DiBartolomeo, Jr.

VIRGINIA BEACH
CAPE CHARLES

FOREWORD

THERE ARE THREE KEY parts to getting ahead in life and business. Your mastery of them will directly affect how far you get. The first two keys are your intellect and your education. They are the very foundation of your advancement. They are certainly necessary but are not sufficient to your full advancement.

Zig Ziglar once said, "You can get anything you want in life if you help enough other people get what they want." The third key to getting ahead in life and business is convincing enough other people to your way of thinking. If you can, you will enjoy a prosperous life. As a speaker working to improve others' lives for over thirty years, I know the best way to convince enough other people to your way of thinking is improving your presentation skills. Doing this is what this book is all about.

Great presentation skills have "opened doors" for me and countless others. They will for you also. So, whether you are trying to convincing your four-year-old to eat his oatmeal, trying to convince a colleague to join your project team, or closing a million dollar real-estate sale, great presentation skills are essential to achieving these goals and any other goals where you are trying to convince anyone of anything.

If you want to greatly improve your presentation skills, this is the book for which you have been waiting. Frank DiBartolomeo has crafted a book jam-packed with ready-to-use tips to significantly improve your interactions with others. If you apply his practical tips and techniques in preparing and delivering presentations, you will be astounded by how quickly you can advance your presentations. You will start hearing comments like, "Boy, that was a great presentation!" "How did you improve your presentations so fast!" and "You answered all my questions and gave me much more information I can use right now!"

After over forty years as a Toastmaster (Distinguished Toastmaster), Air Force Officer, Industry Program Manager, award-winning speaker, and public speaking coach, Frank knows what he is talking about, and more importantly, he knows how to teach you how to do it in this book. Frank is a doer, not just a talker. Over his career, he has significantly influenced military, U.S. government, and industry leaders in their decision making. He has also evaluated hundreds of presentations in helping others propel their lives and careers.

Over my career, I have met hundreds of speaking coaches and trainers. Frank is one of the best. He works with all speakers; however, his specialty is helping technical professionals, including engineers and scientists, inspire, motivate, and influence their customers, colleagues, and stakeholders by improving their presentation skills, communication, and personal presence. His keynotes, workshops, and professional development programs are always a hit.

Buy, read, and take action on the advice in this book. Frank has distilled his vast speaking experience for you in this readable, pertinent, and fun book. After reading this book, you will refer to it time and time again. It will answer all your presentation questions!

Arnold Sanow, MBA, CSP (Certified Speaking Professional), Professional Speaker, Trainer, Presentation Skills Coach, and author of 7 books to include *Present with Power, Punch, and Pizzazz . . . The Ultimate Guide to Delivering Presentations with Poise, Persuasion, and Professionalism*

TABLE OF CONTENTS

DEDICATION

I dedicate this book to my mom and dad, Julia and Frank, my brother John, my wife Elaine, and my four children: Michael, Matthew, Frank, and Jacqueline.

To my mom and dad, Julia and Frank DiBartolomeo, thank you for every ounce of positiveness in me. You were and still are my benchmark for never giving up. You both set a high bar!

To my wife, Elaine, thank you for the life of which husbands can only dream. Thanks for your patience, your wisdom, and your love!

To my brother, John, thank you for your "Rock of Gibraltar" support in my personal and professional life. Talking to you is always a joy!

To my children, Michael, Matthew, Frank, and Jacqueline, thank you for your love, your support, and keeping me grounded in what really matters in life!

I love you all!

INTRODUCTION

HERE'S A LOADED QUESTION. Do you want to advance your career and have a happy life? Did anyone say no? Of course not. We all want to advance our careers and have a happy life, however you define that. Earl Nightingale told us that whatever you want to get in life, you will have to get through other people. Service to others is the key to your career and life. How much you earn right now is directly proportional to the amount of service you are providing to others.

This rule applies whether you are a McDonald's restaurant worker, a lawyer, or a business owner. Great service can make you rich beyond your dreams. Mediocre service will make you live paycheck to paycheck. If you provide bad service, you will find yourself on welfare or, at least, in the unemployment line. So, if everything you want in life depends on others, does it not make sense to improve how we interact with others? Improving your presentation skills will greatly improve your interaction with others and literally positively add to your paycheck, bank account, and, most important, your self-esteem.

We have established that improving your presentation skills is vital to your career and happiness. Then why aren't more people improving this key skill? Well, there are two challenges facing you in improving your presentation skills. The first challenge is to realize that improving your skills will advance your life. This may sound like everyone should know this. But most people do not or, at least, they do not think about it enough to improve their presentation skills. This, believe it or not, is the hardest challenge to improving your skills. This reluctance to improve your skills in this area is enough to preclude the next challenge from being overcome.

The second challenge is putting in the time to study and practice to really improve your presentation skills. I am going to make a blanket statement that I believe is always true. I believe anyone, no matter their station in life or other life factors, can improve their presentation skills to become the best speaker they can be and, thus, improve their lives beyond their wildest dreams.

In the early 1990s, I took an adult education course at the local high school to learn how to play the piano. This may sound like duh, but I soon realized I needed a piano to practice. A similar thing happens with improving your presentation skills. Except the piano has been replaced by speaking opportunities. You need regular speaking opportunities to practice speaking in front of an audience. Think about joining your local Toastmasters Club. Dues are inexpensive, and the return on monetary investment is huge.

By the way, I bought a piano and became a passable piano player, which I still am because that is where I am satisfied. I did not have to become a concert pianist.

Improving your presentation skills will have an immediate effect on your career and your life the minute you start improving your skills and start proving it to yourself in front of an audience. There is nothing quite like the spectacular feeling a speaker gets after he or she has given a speech to an applauding audience.

I wrote this book for the person who wants to be a passable speaker, the person who wants to speak for a living, and the person who wants to become a "concert pianist" of speaking. So, this book is for John Smith, passable speaker; Mary Jane Robinson, professional speaker; or Les Brown, legendary motivational speaker. It has something for everyone at whatever level you are or want to attain.

The book is divided into six parts.

- **Part I: Speaking in Public: Why it is Important.** This part is at the "fifty thousand–foot level." I talk about the importance of speaking greatly, how important good writing is to good speaking, how you gain power from positive speaking, developing the will to prepare to give a great presentation, how power words ignite your presentations and make them memorable for your audience, and how cool heads and great speaking are needed in times of crisis.
- **Part II: Speech Development—General.** If Part I is at the "fifty thousand–foot level," Part II is at the "twenty thousand–foot level." I talk about what to do when you are asked to speak, how to develop a presentation quickly, how to connect with your audience, how to make your presentations compelling to your audience, how putting less content in your presentation has a greater impact on your audience, how to make your presentation "crystal clear" to your audience, what to do after you have your presentation topic, the one ingredient absolutely indispensable to your presentation, how adversity reveals great speaking tips, and presentation "pain points."

- **Part III: Speech Development.** If Part I is at the "fifty thousand–foot level" and Part II is at the "twenty thousand–foot level," then Part III is at the "five hundred–foot level." In Part III, I get down into the nitty gritty of presentation preparation. I cover how power words ignite your presentations and make them memorable for your audience, how to grab your audience with great openings, how common speech errors can derail your presentation and what to do about it, speaking secrets of a great speaker, the positive effect of adding stories to your presentation and how to do it, and the magic effect on your audience of speech patterns.

- **Part IV: Speech Delivery.** We take another "five hundred–foot level" journey in Part IV. It covers dressing for success, how to keep great eye contact, how not to fall into the "Apology Trap," how to field audience questions with aplomb, what to do when things go wrong in your presentation, how to make your great listening feed your great speaking, and how to establish and maintain great credibility with your audience.

- **Part V: The Future of Speaking.** Part V covers the particulars of speaking virtually to include why virtual speaking's time is now, how to stay connected by speaking virtually, and how to use technology to enhance your presentation.

- **Part VI: Presentation Tips for Specific Speaking Situations.** Parts I to Part V explore all parts of speaking and provide you with many tips, tools, and techniques to greatly improve your presentations. However, there are specific situations that require more guidance. These include delivering a keynote presentation, chairing a meeting, facilitating a meeting, being a master of ceremonies, and presenting training. Part VI provides guidance for these specific speaking situations as a chronology of what to do before, during, and after the event.

It would be extremely hard to overestimate how much great presentation skills will positively affect your career trajectory. Remember, Earl Nightingale told us that whatever you want to get in life, you will have to get through other people.

Imagine you are talking before 20,356 people in the Capital One Arena in downtown Washington, DC. Imagine the event has a waiting list to get in. Imagine the emcee introducing you. Imagine the thunderous applause from the audience. Imagine walking to the lectern and putting down your notes on it. Imagine starting your presentation with a pertinent, heartfelt story. Imagine hitting your main points and reciting relevant stories that pull at the emotions of the audience. Imagine the thunderous applause when you are done. Imagine walking to the wings of the stage. Imagine hearing the audience cheer when you cannot see them anymore. Imagine the great memory you now have of this night!

Some of you are saying this could never be me. Well, anyone famous was once an unknown, as is illustrated by the following person:

- Lost job, 1832
- Defeated for legislature, 1832
- Failed in business, 1833
- Elected to legislature, 1834
- Sweetheart (Ann Rutledge) died, 1835
- Had nervous breakdown, 1836
- Defeated for Speaker, 1838
- Defeated for nomination for Congress, 1843
- Elected to Congress, 1846
- Lost re-nomination, 1848

- Rejected for Land Officer, 1849
- Defeated for Senate, 1854
- Defeated for nomination for Vice President, 1856
- Again, defeated for Senate, 1858
- Elected President, 1860

Of course, I am talking about Abraham Lincoln. He was not highly regarded for the majority of his life. See what he accomplished by not giving up. You may not become President of the United States, but would you settle to become the best speaker you can be?

Earl Nightingale said, "Luck is when preparedness meets opportunity." So prepare yourself to be a great speaker by reading this book and take action on what it says, so when your opportunity comes, and it always will, you will be ready for your star to shine!

Read this book, internalize its advice, and then take action to make what it says happen in your life. You might not be the next Abraham Lincoln, but you could be the next Les Brown!

Anyone can become a much better speaker than they are now. ***YOU CAN DO IT!***

PART I: SPEAKING IN PUBLIC: WHY IS IT IMPORTANT?

WHY IS BEING ABLE to speak in public important? Since prehistoric times when language came about, human beings have been trying to convince other human beings to their way of thinking. We see it in our schools, our politics, and our homes, along with a million other places. It is the stuff of human communication discourse. It defines us as human beings.

We admire the great speakers who cause us to think, change our viewpoint, and dream of what we can become: the inspiring pastor, the encouraging father or mother, the emboldening teacher. We look up to them. We emulate them. We seek their wisdom.

This is the power of the spoken word. It moves us, inspires us, and causes us to take action to better our lives, the lives of our families, and maybe most importantly, the lives of others. In a literal sense, it is responsible for all human achievement since the dawn of human history.

Part I of this book speaks to this importance of public speaking. It talks about:

- Speak Greatly to Lead Greatly!
- Great Writing = Great Speaking!
- Speak Positive – Gain Power!
- Do You Have the Will to Prepare to Win?
- Speak Greatly in Times of Crisis!
- Are You a Go-Giver Speaker?
- Where Are You on the Speaker's Hierarchy of Needs?
- So Where Can I Speak?
- As a Speaker, Do You Have an Attitude of Gratitude?

SPEAK GREATLY TO LEAD GREATLY!

*"The greatest danger for most of us is not that our aim
is too high and we miss it, but that it is too low
and we reach it."*

—Michelangelo

IS GREAT SPEAKING ESSENTIAL to great leading? Think about it. Can you think of any great leader who was not a great speaker? Great leaders use their great speaking ability to influence their followers. Because of this, great speaking is indeed essential to great leading.

Below you will find out how great speaking significantly enhances your leadership in the following qualities: integrity, resolution, and having the strength of their convictions.

GREAT SPEAKING IS INTEGRAL TO DEVELOPING UNQUESTIONED INTEGRITY

Earl Nightingale in his audio album *Lead the Field* talks of an American Army General captured in the Korean War. He was subjected to all types of physical torture, solitary confinement, and sleep deprivation. The general was ordered several times to sign a confession admitting he was a spy for the United States. He refused every time.

Integrity

One day, his captors told him if he did not sign the confession by daybreak, he would be executed. Thinking he was going to be executed the next day, he wrote a letter to his wife that night. In the letter, he wrote, "Tell Johnny the word is integrity."

The general was later repatriated to the United States in a prisoner exchange. But thinking he would be executed the next morning, he asked his wife to tell their son, Johnny, the word is integrity. What would be your last words on this earth to your son or daughter? These would be the words you want them to remember through life. Would it be the word integrity?

Dictionary.com (www.dictionary.com) defines integrity as "adherence to moral and ethical principles; soundness of moral character; honesty." I was pondering this the other day and thought how your public speaking greatly supports your integrity.

You are your most convincing to your audience when you adhere to high moral and ethical principles. How can you do this as a speaker? Prepare your own presentation, and when you use someone else's words, attribute them. It is entirely appropriate to support your presentation with quotes from other speakers if, and only if, you attribute the words to the rightful speaker.

**

Integrity is the bedrock of your speaking life. Modern audiences are incredibly perceptive and can catch when a speaker is being less than honest with them. Your integrity or lack of your integrity will be obvious to your audience.

Adherence to high integrity will bring you much appreciation from your audiences. In addition to integrity, audiences are looking for leaders that are resolute.

GREAT SPEAKING SIGNIFICANTLY ENHANCES A LEADER'S RESOLUTION

George Washington is a perfect example of the resolute leader. He agreed to lead a ragtag group of farmers, merchants, and part-time militiamen in a struggle for independence against the most powerful military on the face of the earth at the time: Great Britain.

George Washington was a man of few words. He never wrote a book and wrote few letters. However, after the War for Independence was won, he led the Constitutional Convention in 1787, which established the Constitution of the United States, which we still live under today. In his capacity as the President of the Constitutional Convention, he had many opportunities to speak to his fellow delegates about the eventual shape of the United States.

Why do you as a speaker need to be as resolute as George Washington? Dictionary.com defines resolute as firmly resolved or determined; set in purpose or opinion; characterized by firmness and determination, as the temper, spirit, actions.

Do you as a speaker have to firmly resolve what you are going to say in your presentations? Do you as a speaker have to have determination to prepare and deliver your speech? Do you as a speaker have to have a strong opinion on what the audience should do with what you are presenting them? I hope you answered a resounding "yes" to all of these questions. This enhances your leadership.

Final question: Are you now convinced you a leader when you are speaking? I hope you answered yes, because people in the audience are following you because you are influencing them through your ideas in your presentation. When you speak, you are a leader.

Integrity and resolution are key attributes of speakers and, therefore, leaders, but people will not follow you if you don't have the strength of your convictions.

GREAT SPEAKING IS ESSENTIAL TO DEVELOPING THE STRENGTH OF YOUR CONVICTIONS

Would you follow a person who makes a decision and then vacillates on that decision? Of course you wouldn't. To gain and retain people's trust in you as a leader, you must follow through on your decisions with the caveat that if further information proves the decision to be a poor one, you are willing to change the decision. Leaders require the strength of their convictions. Great public speaking skills significantly add to your strength of convictions.

It's ironic that it takes sometimes many years to build a reputation of which you can be proud. However, it takes much less time to lose that reputation if you show yourself unworthy and even a longer time to regain a great reputation if that is possible.

General Dwight David Eisenhower was the commander of the

D-Day invasion, Army Chief of Staff, and President of the United States. In planning and then executing the D-Day invasion of France and destroying the Nazi war machine, he is a prime example of the leader who had the strength of his convictions.

General George C. Marshall, Army Chief of Staff in World War II, chose General Eisenhower over more senior generals to lead the D-Day invasion. Why? General Marshall knew that the person leading the invasion would have to have the strength of his convictions to bring together a coalition of many nations to defeat Nazi Germany. General Eisenhower is a great example of how to use your speaking ability to influence others to your way of thinking.

Another great example from the American Civil War is General Ulysses S. Grant. Up until the time General Grant was appointed the commanding general of the Union forces, President Abraham Lincoln went through a number of commanding generals that vacillated and let the Confederate forces escape many times.

General Robert E. Lee, the commanding general of the Confederate forces, knew that his forces would survive until the Union could field a general with the strength of his convictions and continuously pursue Confederate forces. That general was Ulysses S. Grant.

From the time he took command, his Union forces relentlessly pursued the Confederate forces until attrition caused General Lee and the Confederate forces to surrender. General Grant would not have been successful unless he could communicate his convictions through clear and unambiguous orders to defeat the Confederacy.

***

Do you think George Washington, Dwight Eisenhower, or Ulysses S. Grant would have been great leaders without the ability to move the men under them (AKA audiences) and the world through their spoken word? The answer to this question is NO.

If you aspire to be a great leader, an essential skill you need to develop is to speak intelligently and convincingly to influence your followers (AKA your audience) to your way of thinking.

With this skill, you will become a master at speaking, leading, and succeeding!

CALL TO ACTION

- Be truthful in all your personal and business dealings.
- Never, never, never give up.
- Increase your resolution by being a person of your convictions.

"I am not afraid of an army of lions led by a sheep; I am afraid of an army of sheep led by a lion."

—Alexander the Great

GREAT WRITING = GREAT SPEAKING!

"If you can't write your message in a sentence, you can't say it in an hour."

—Dianna Daniels Booher

VIEWING THE TITLE OF this chapter, you may be saying, "Of course writing well helps us to speak well." However, have you ever taken the time to really think why this is so? Hopefully, this chapter will encourage you to write more and discover the vein of gold between your ears.

In this chapter, we will explore three reasons why your writing will actually improve your public speaking: writing helps you clarify your thinking, reduces your anxiety, and "mines" your thoughts for the material in your presentations.

WRITING HELPS YOU CLARIFY YOUR THINKING

There are thousands of thoughts that pass through your brain every day. Some of those thoughts will literally make you a million bucks if you can capture and develop them.

Have you ever had a really great thought that would be a great idea for a new business or improve your relationship with your daughter or solve that seemingly unsolvable problem at work? Then, in the next minute after that thought, the thought is fuzzy to you and fading fast until eventually you cannot remember the essence of or even the thought itself?

There is an old Chinese proverb, "The palest ink is better than the best memory." What writing does for your speaking is it allows you to see your words in "black and white." You can arrange and rearrange your words until you are satisfied with the way they sound. This is especially easy to do through your computer word processor.

The Cards on the Wall exercise is a great example of how writing helps you clarify your thinking when it comes to your speaking. So, what is the Cards on the Wall exercise? In Cards on the Wall, you write each topic idea you generate on a separate Post-it note ("yellow sticky") and then logically group them on a board. After all your ideas are on the board, you will magically start seeing patterns of your ideas emerging. These patterns become the main points of your presentation. Use Cards on the Wall and you will never lack for main points for your presentations.

An added benefit of writing is it actually lowers your anxiety.

WRITING HELPS TO REDUCE YOUR ANXIETY

I am not a psychologist, but I do know that a great way to relieve anxiety concerning your presentations is to keep a journal. Why is this so? A large part of anxiety in preparing your presentations is due to having all these ideas flowing in your "grey cells" with no "traffic cop" to ensure there are no collisions. Your writing is the "traffic cop."

Quite often, you may be thinking you are not accomplishing much while you are preparing your presentations. This increases your anxiety and actually sabotages your "creative juices." Writing out your presentation can give you a great sense of accomplishing something, which will reduce your stress concerning your presentation.

You can choose to write out the words or write bullets for the main ideas. The bullets are what is on the cards in the Cards on the Wall exercise.

Writing the actual words or bullets of your presentation early in your preparation process will improve your disposition, reduce your stress, and encourage you to finish the task of creating your presentation. Try this. After you have done some writing for your presentation, ask those you love whether you seem more relaxed, more pleasant, and more willing to help others. The answer will be a resounding YES!

In addition to writing your presentation causing you clarify your thoughts and lessen your anxiety, an additional benefit is it helps you to "mine" your thoughts for ideas that might or might not make it into your presentation. The key here is to get a lot of ideas on paper where you can then "separate the wheat from the chaff."

WRITING WELL HELPS YOU TO "MINE" YOUR THOUGHTS

I talked previously about benefits of keeping a daily journal. Because you are a speaker, keeping a journal has the added benefit of recording your thoughts that will more often than not be fleeting if you don't write them down. Jeanne Robertson wrote a whole book on this called *Don't Let the Funny Stuff Get Away!*

Don't make the mistake of thinking an idea has to be immediately applied to a presentation you have in the works. The best writers know that thoughts that pop into your head are not immediately applicable to something they are writing. It is the same with you.

As a speaker, you should keep a daily journal where you can document all your fleeting thoughts so they will not be lost. These ideas become the kernels of your future presentations or can add greatly to your current presentation projects.

Earl Nightingale says, "Writing down your ideas when you get them is like mining in a vein of pure gold. Your mind is that and much more." He goes on to say that startling things happen when you roll your ideas on the rotisserie of your mind. How's that for symbolism?

You should periodically read through your journal. An idea in your journal may be applicable to one of your presentation projects now, whereas a month ago when you recorded it in your daily journal, it wasn't.

***

In this chapter, we have explored three reasons why your writing will actually improve your public speaking: writing helps you clarify your thinking, reduce your anxiety, and "mines" your thoughts for the material in your present and future presentations.

Write down the ideas in your head. They provide a treasure trove of material for a whole host of your presentations. You will be glad you did!

CALL TO ACTION

- Thoughts are fleeting; writing is permanent. Make a promise with yourself this week to write down your thoughts and then analyze them to see if you are on the right track.
- Don't worry about forgetting something you need to do. Make a list of these activities.
- Think on paper; "mine" your mind.

"You can always edit a bad page.
You can't edit a blank page."

—Jodi Picoult

SPEAK POSITIVE – GAIN POWER!

"You become what you think about."

—Earl Nightingale

I WAS LISTENING TO a speaker the other day. His main premise was there is no reason to be positive when there is so much wrong with our world today. According to him, you can't "just drink some hot chocolate and expect everything to work out." He, obviously, did not know much about the power of positive thinking. It is so sad to see a person of influence talk this way.

You have great power within you to uplift your audiences to change their thoughts to positive ones and to help them create great lives for themselves.

This chapter will cover three ways the power of your positive speaking can help others to improve their lives: (1) be a model of positiveness when you are speaking, (2) give your audiences the practical actions to increase their positive attitude, and (3) "recharge your batteries" by reading the great positive thinking books to maintain your positive attitude.

BE A MODEL OF POSITIVENESS

People come to hear you speak to be uplifted, learn something new, and be entertained. Yes, great speaking is entertaining also. Your audiences want to feel better about themselves when they leave your presentations than they felt when they entered the presentation venue.

The best way to be a positive role model is to read books that inspire you (more on this later), talk to people who encourage you to improve, and watch videos that can teach you how to transform your presentations.

I think you already know things don't always go the way you want them to at your presentations. I was giving a presentation to sixty people a few weeks ago in a hall, and the lapel microphone would not work. As a consequence, I had to project more, and a few times, I had to ask the last row of the audience whether they could hear me. By the way, every speaker, whether you have a booming voice or not, should be speaking into a microphone. If you don't use a microphone, you will not have a voice the next day. The audience will be glad you did use a microphone.

When things don't turn out exactly right at your presentations, shrug it off and remain positive. Remember, you are the model. The best way to remain positive is to have backup plans for when the lapel microphone doesn't work, the projector used for your presentation does not project, and the DVD player with that vital video doesn't function correctly.

It is okay to give theories about positive thinking to audiences, but what will help your audiences more is to give them practical actions they can do to increase their positive attitude.

GIVE YOUR AUDIENCES PRACTICAL ACTIONS TO INCREASE THEIR POSITIVE ATTITUDE

POSITIVE ENERGY

Have you ever attended a presentation and wondered afterward as to how you can use the information in the presentation to better your personal and professional life? Always, always, always give your audience a call to action at the end of your presentation.

The tools I am about to give you come from *The Power of Positive Thinking* by Dr. Norman Vincent Peale (1952), *Think and Grow Rich* by Napoleon Hill (1937), and *The Magic of Thinking Big* by Dr. David J. Schwartz (1959), three books that have made a huge difference in my life. In the next section, I give you a glimpse into these self-development classics. However, for now, let's look at three success actions you can give to your audiences to increase their positive attitude.

Thoughts Follow Actions. I think you will agree that your actions follow your thoughts. However, have you ever considered that your thoughts can also follow your actions?

So how can this help you give increasingly better presentations? For one thing, if you are not feeling confident about your presentation, acting confident will actually begin to increase your confidence. It sounds hokey, but it is true.

If you are feeling disorganized in your presentation, use the action of rearranging your presentation outline to better organize your presentation to decrease its disorganization.

If you are fearful about giving your presentation, use the action of seeking more information about your audience. This will create the thought that your presentation is highly relevant to your audience and will increase your positive attitude.

The Power of Persistence. My son Frankie is an Eagle Scout. I am very proud of him. At his Eagle Scout Court of Honor (ceremony conferring the Eagle Scout rank in Boy Scouts) a number of years ago, I delivered a presentation about persistence, his persistence specifically that directly contributed to his becoming an Eagle Scout. In that presentation, I quoted President Calvin Coolidge, which I think sums up completely why persistence is an absolutely essential ingredient to your success:

> *"Nothing in this world can take the place of persistence. Talent will not: nothing is more common than unsuccessful men with talent. Genius will not; unrewarded genius is almost a proverb. Education will not: the world is full of educated derelicts. Persistence and determination alone are omnipotent."*

Goals Turn Your Dreams into Your Reality. Look around your home, your neighborhood, and your world. Have you ever thought whatever you see was once not there? Everything you see started with a thought in someone's mind—everything! Everything includes famous landmarks like the Eiffel Tower in Paris, Saint Peter's Basilica in Rome, the Golden Gate Bridge in San Francisco, and not so famous things like your car, the local supermarket, and the color you painted your daughter's room. All these realities started with a single thought. Goals are what are responsible for accomplishing them.

Around every Wednesday, my wife, Elaine, and I start putting together a list of tasks to accomplish over the following weekend. This list contains our goals for the weekend, what we want to achieve in the two days off from work. A funny thing, though: when the list had twenty things on it, few of the goals were accomplished. We found out that if the list had only three goals, the absolutes we needed to get done always were. So keep the list of goals you are working on short, whether that is three, four, or five goals. It is amazing, but you will get all of them done.

"RECHARGE YOUR BATTERIES" BY READING THE GREAT POSITIVE THINKING BOOKS

Like you, I have had great and not so great periods in my life. We all need some help, every once in a while, to bring us up when we are down. If you are not positive when you are speaking to your audiences, I guarantee your presentation will fall flat. So it is important to "recharge your batteries" so you can be the most positive you can be.

Because you are a speaker, I bet you are a reader also. There are three incredible books that have been and still are a great positive influence on my life: *The Power of Positive Thinking* by Dr. Norman Vincent Peale (1952), *Think and Grow Rich* by Napoleon Hill (1937), and *The Magic of Thinking Big* by Dr. David J. Schwartz (1959).

As you can see, the newest book of the three is over sixty years old, which, hopefully, tells you that wisdom does not become irrelevant with age.

The Power of Positive Thinking by Dr. Norman Vincent Peale was a lifeline for me when I needed it. It has chapters entitled, "Believe in Yourself," "How to Create Your Own Happiness," and

"Expect the Best and Get It." To quote the back cover of the book, it is "a practical, direct-action, personal-improvement manual." If you think you have reached your plateau of achievement, read this book and you will realize that plateau is just your "base camp" and the summit of your achievement is still in your future. Read this book and tear down your "internal prisons" to achieve your dreams!

Think and Grow Rich by Napoleon Hill is a classic of self-development and success. It started becoming a reality a few years into the twentieth century when Andrew Carnegie, the steel magnate, commissioned Napoleon Hill, at the time a journalist, to chronicle the common success traits of men of great wealth and achievement at the time, such as Henry Ford, Alexander Graham Bell, and John D. Rockefeller.

Mr. Hill talks of desire as being "the starting point of all achievement," persistence as "an essential factor in the procedure of transmuting desire into its monetary equivalent," and the power of the mastermind being the "coordinating of knowledge and effort, in a spirit of harmony, between two or more people, for the attainment of a definite purpose."

The Magic of Thinking Big by Dr. David J. Schwartz is another classic of self-development and success. From the back cover of the book, "Dr. Schwartz proves that you don't need to be an intellectual or have innate talent to attain great success and satisfaction—but you do need to learn and understand the habit of thinking and behaving in ways that will get you there." Chapters include, "Believe You Can Succeed and You Will," "Cure Yourself of Excusitis, the Failure Disease," and "You Are What You Think You Are."

Read these books, internalize them, put their contents to work in your life, and you and others will be amazed at the positive difference it will make in your life and the lives of your audiences.

***

The three ways the power of your positive speaking can help others to improve their lives are: (1) be a model of positiveness when you are speaking, (2) give your audiences the practical actions to increase their positive attitudes, and (3) "recharge your batteries" by reading the great positive thinking books to maintain your positive attitude.

So go forth, be positive, and spread positive thinking in our world.

CALL TO ACTION

- Be uplifting to yourself and others. Remember positive thoughts follow positive action.
- Give your colleagues and friends positive ways to increase their positive attitudes like speaking about solutions to challenges instead of problems at work or in their personal lives.
- Feed your mind with positive reading like *The Power of Positive Thinking* like you fill your body with positive food.

"The greatest discovery of my generation is that human beings can alter their lives by altering their attitudes of mind."

—William James

DO YOU HAVE THE WILL TO PREPARE TO WIN?

"I've missed more than nine thousand shots in my career. I've lost almost three hundred games. Twenty-six times, I've been trusted to take the game winning shot and missed. I've failed over and over and over again in my life. And that is why I succeed."

—Michael Jordan

THE LEGENDARY COACH OF the Alabama Crimson Tide football team, Paul "Bear" Bryant, once said, "It's not the will to win that matters—everyone has that. It's the will to prepare to win that matters." Bear Bryant won six national collegiate football championships. Not only that, his legacy lived on after he stepped down as head coach. Subsequently, Alabama won six additional national collegiate football championships. I would say he knew how to produce winners.

The will to prepare to win. What does this have to do with public speaking? Everything!

Over my long engineering career, I have seen many technical people prepare for presentations like this: develop the PowerPoint slides right up to the time before the presentation and then deliver the presentation. They then wonder why the presentation missed the mark.

They are making a fundamental mistake that the vast majority of technical speakers make. The presentation is not just the slides. The slides support the presentation, not the other way around. The delivery is the presentation because that is what the audience sees, hears, and feels.

The problem is very few technical presenters take the time to practice the delivery of the presentation, which is what will have impact with the audience. The first step is realizing that you need to practice the presentation delivery.

Below are three tips to greatly aid you in practicing your presentation delivery.

- ***Speak ideas and not words***. Now what do I mean by this? I prepare my presentations by writing bullets of ideas instead of full sentences and paragraphs. I try to make the bullets as short as possible so I will not be tempted to read them while at the same time making the bullets long enough so I can remember the thought I want to express. Some presenters want to start with writing complete sentences and paragraphs, and that is fine as long as this is just a start. But if they are not turned into bullets before you finish practicing your delivery, you will be strongly tempted to remember the exact words you have written. And reciting exact words usually leads to presentation turn-offs such as speaking in a monotone amongst others.

-  ***Practice your presentation delivery by yourself in front of a mirror first***. You may feel uncomfortable doing this, but you will quickly see first-hand all the annoying gestures, ticks, and mannerisms you do when you are presenting. Jettison these annoying parts of your delivery as quickly as you can. Practicing your presentation in front of a mirror also allows you to practice meaningful and relevant gestures. Body language is a large part of your communicating with your audience. If you do not use gestures in your presentation delivery, you will never become the great speaker you want to be.

-  Now comes the frightening part. ***Practice your presentation delivery in front of a live audience of trusted colleagues and friends.*** I say trusted, because you do not want them to say your presentation is great if it is not. Suggest the "sandwich" method of evaluation. Have each one of your practice audience members say something positive about your talk, something you can improve, and then something motivational to encourage you to improve your delivery.

Remember, your will to prepare to win includes practicing your presentation delivery speaking ideas and not words, practicing in front of a mirror, and, finally, practicing in front of trusted colleagues and friends.

There is no sure thing in this world, but practicing your delivery comes very close because the payoff of a great presentation delivery is worth it.

CALL TO ACTION

- Speak ideas and not words during your presentations.
- Practice your presentation delivery in front of mirror before you present to anyone else.
- Seek feedback like your life depends on it.

"If you have an important point to make, don't try to be subtle or clever. Use a pile driver. Hit the point once. Then come back and hit it again. Then hit it a third time—a tremendous whack."

—Winston Churchill

SPEAK GREATLY IN TIMES OF CRISIS!

"Your present circumstances don't determine where you can go; they merely determine where you can start."

—Nido Qubein

THIS CHAPTER WILL FOCUS on the need for great speaking in times of crisis. Great speaking by parents to their children. Great speaking by our government's officials to their constituents. Great speaking by us to our work colleagues, relatives, and friends.

How should you speak in times of crisis? Below are some points you may want to consider.

DON'T DIMINISH PEOPLE'S FEARS

I learned a long time ago in a trial I had in my life that our feelings are neither right nor wrong; they just are. You and I are complex beings with our hereditary traits and environmental influences all rolled up into who we are. After considering family traits and environmental influences, you are truly unique. There never was and never will be a person exactly like you.

When we speak to someone who is fearful in times of crisis, what is your first reaction? Do you validate his or her fear or do you say something like, "Oh, it is really not that bad." Remember, being scared is a feeling, and I just mentioned above that feelings are neither right nor wrong. They just are. Validate the fear in others as a real and justified feeling.

I went to undergraduate school in Newark, New Jersey. My college was in the central ward of Newark where some of the Vietnam riots occurred in the 1960s. My undergraduate days were not too long after the Vietnam War. There were times when I was fearful, but I did not let my fear overtake me. Denis Waitley says, "Fear stands for False Reality Appearing Real." I now know many years later the fear I felt was false reality. But at the time, it seemed very real. Don't discount the fear of others. Help them work through their fear.

As a side note, in all fairness, Newark today is a fine city that has been rejuvenated by several mayors and New Jersey governors. I often say I am going to visit the campus, and I will someday soon.

Fear is real and justifiable to the people who are feeling it. When you speak to fearful people, be empathetic toward them and help them work through their fear.

Being positive without discounting the fear felt by others goes a long way to resolving the situation, but it is not enough when people are going through a crisis. You must talk of solutions and not problems.

TALK OF SOLUTIONS, NOT PROBLEMS

 What kind of a world would we live in if George Washington succumbed to the British Army? What kind of world would we live in if President Lincoln had not preserved the Union? What kind of world would we live in if Thomas Edison had not invented the incandescent light bulb?

These three men encountered obstacles that would stop most men and women in their tracks. But they refused to succumb to negativity. They always talked of how to solve the problem at hand. Don't get me wrong. They had their bouts with despair. The difference is they rose to the occasion by working through their fear to a solution.

Walt Disney was known to say, "If ten people tell me my idea will not work, I will immediately start work on it." Can anyone out there refute the "Disney Magic?"

People are drawn to those who talk of solutions. Mind you, the solutions have to be plausible. When you are proposing a solution in your presentations, be ready to answer the following questions: "Why is it important to the audience?" "What do you want the audience to do different to make what you are saying a reality?"

You know fear is real and justifiable to the people who are feeling it. When you speak to fearful people, be empathetic and help them work through their fear.

You also know being positive without discounting the fear felt by others goes a long way to resolving the situation, but you must talk of solutions and not problems.

Finally, in a crisis, we need to inspire in people a "Can Do" attitude, giving them specific actions they can take to lessen the impact of the crisis.

INSPIRE A "CAN DO" ATTITUDE AND ACTIONS

It was June 5, 1940. The Nazis had overrun the Netherlands, Belgium, and France in six weeks. It was obvious the next country in the Nazis' sights was Great Britain. On this day, Winston Churchill in a speech to Parliament said this: "We shall fight on the seas and oceans. We shall fight with growing confidence and growing strength in the air. We shall defend our island whatever the cost may be. We shall fight on the beaches. We shall fight on the landing grounds. We shall fight in the fields and the streets. We shall fight in the hills. We shall never surrender!"

In 1954, the wartime correspondent Edward R. Murrow said of Churchill's inspiring speeches, "He mobilized the English language and sent it into battle."

No one can refute the effect of Churchill's inspiring speech to Parliament and his future speeches. He inspired a war effort that saved a nation from extinction.

Hopefully, you are not faced with a challenge of this magnitude. Just the same, as a speaker, you may be put in the position of inspiring others to put forth the required effort to defeat the challenge.

The challenge may be your child has cancer or you are suddenly without a job or the death of a spouse.

Whatever the challenge may be, remember, you sometimes cannot control your circumstances, but you can always control your response to those circumstances.

I am not a psychiatrist or psychologist, but I believe worry, fear, and panic cut off your mental processes needed to solve or lesson the crisis at hand. As Norman Vincent Peale says, "A calm mind generates power."

A calm mind also generates a "Can Do" attitude focused on solutions and not problems. When you speak to others going through a crisis, inspire this "Can Do" attitude in them. Also, give them actions they can take to alleviate or lesson the crisis.

***

Now you know how to speak to others in times of crisis. Being positive without discounting the fear felt by others goes a long way to resolving the situation. Talk of solutions and not problems to others. And, finally, inspire in people a "Can Do" attitude, giving them specific actions they can take to lessen the impact of the crisis.

History has shown us great speaking is needed in times of crisis!

CALL TO ACTION

- Validate the fear you see in yourself and others. Work through your fear.
- Talk of solutions, not problems.
- Inspire a "Can Do" attitude in yourself and others like Winston Churchill did.

"Seeds of faith are always within us; sometimes it takes a crisis to nourish and encourage their growth."

—Susan L. Taylor

ARE YOU A GO-GIVER SPEAKER?

"For it is in giving that we receive."
—St. Francis of Assisi

I **ATTENDED THE NATIONAL** Speakers Association Washington, DC Area Chapter Auction one year. You might imagine the types of items up to bid on at a speaking group auction: electronic doo-dads used by speakers, three hours with premier speaking business coaches, and of course speaking books.

I won a stack of speaking books. You might think I immediately went home and devoured each book in order. Well, I didn't. At the time I was in graduate school, and after school I was in the process of building the foundation for my business.

It wasn't until I was perusing my substantial collection of leadership, self-development, and speaking books that I came across a book entitled *The Go-Giver: A Little Story About a Powerful Business Idea* by Bob Burg and John David Mann.

It was an eye-opener. You have probably heard the expression, "When the student is ready, the teacher will appear." I was the student, and this book was my teacher. I was trying to get smarter on networking, and this book "rang a bell" for me.

It is the story of Joe, a go-getter, and how he is taught by a wise man named Pindar why it makes relationship and business sense to replace his "go-getter" ways with "go-giver" ways. Through this story, the authors introduce five laws of the "go-giver." We will explore these five laws briefly to see how they apply to our speaking profession.

***

The Law of Value: Your true worth is determined by how much more you give in value than you take in payment.

We all admire the person who goes the "extra mile." You've probably heard the expression, "There are no traffic jams on the extra mile." Working in this "extra mile" deepens and strengthens the relationships between you and the people you serve. The people you serve are a large part of your speaking business network. The depth and strength of your relationships are directly proportional to the depth and strength and success of your career and business.

The next law concerns how your income is determined.

***

The Law of Compensation: Your income is determined by how many people you serve and how well you serve them.

If you are in a speaking business, your income is determined by how well you serve your customers, because if you serve them well, they will keep coming back for more and tell others about your great service, which makes a good portion of these new people new customers. Serving your customers superbly is your best marketing plan.

The next law concerns how to expand your influence with others.

***

The Law of Influence: Your influence is determined by how abundantly you place other people's interests first.

The analogy here for speakers is always put the interests of your audience first. The way to do this is present information that is important to them and they can immediately use. Audience members attend a lot of presentations where it is obvious when the speaker has not done his or her homework to find out what the audience knows, wants to hear, and needs to hear about the topic. So it is obvious when speakers do their homework on the audience. Do your homework on your audience and expand your influence.

The next law concerns sharing your most valuable gift.

***

The Law of Authenticity: The most valuable gift you have to offer is yourself.

No one has ever been or will be exactly like you. Whether you speak in your business or speak on your job, if you are not yourself when you speak, you will have a credibility problem. Audiences have a sixth sense when speakers are not acting true to themselves. You are giving a gift to your audience when you are yourself. Don't hide yourself under a rock!

The final law concerns your openness to receiving from others.

***

The Law of Receptivity: The key to effective giving is to stay open to receiving.

The book *The Go-giver* talks about what we are taught from infancy: "It is better to give than to receive." Is it? From the book, "All the giving in the world won't bring success, won't create the results you want, unless you also make yourself willing and able to receive in like measure. Because if you don't let yourself receive, you're refusing the gifts of others and you shut down the flow." Aid the "flow" by accepting gifts from others graciously. An example of receptivity for you as a speaker means accepting the gift of feedback from others about our speaking. They're gifts you should accept. How else will you improve?

***

Are you a "go-giver" speaker? Do you give more in value than in payment? Do you realize your income is determined by how many people you serve and how well you serve them? Do you abundantly place other people's interests first? Do you give the gift of yourself to others? Are you open to receiving from others?

If you answered "no" to any of these questions, you know what you have to do.

Practice being a "go-giver" speaker and make the world a better place for all of us!

CALL TO ACTION

- Strive to give others more in value than you are paid.
- Increase your income by increasing the number of others you serve better.
- Put other people's interest first and create an "army" of people looking out for your interest.

"No one has ever become poor by giving."

—Anne Frank

WHERE ARE YOU ON THE SPEAKER'S HIERARCHY OF NEEDS?

"If you plan on being anything less than you are capable of being, you will probably be unhappy all the days of your life."

—Abraham Maslow

SOME OF YOU MAY be familiar with Abraham Maslow's Hierarchy of Needs. Maslow postulated that all humans have the same needs, which can be represented by a prioritized pyramid of in ascending order the following needs: Physiological, Safety, Belongingness and Love, Esteem, and Self-Actualization. Maslow's prioritized needs is pictorially shown below.

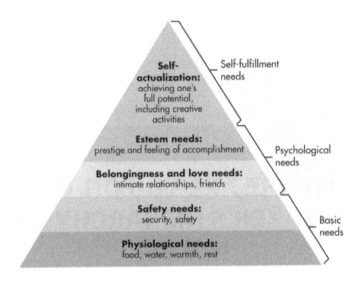

Before you can satisfy your Safety Needs of security and safety, you have to satisfy your Physiological Needs of food, water, warmth, and rest.

Before you can satisfy your Belongingness and Love Needs of intimate relationships and friends, you have to satisfy your Safety Needs of security and safety, and so on.

I posit to you just like Maslow's Hierarchy of Needs, there is a Speaker's Hierarchy of Needs. In fact, you are, right now, somewhere on your personal Speaker's Hierarchy of Needs.

The Speaker's Hierarchy of Needs from lowest need to highest need are Speaker Security Needs, Speaker Belongingness Needs, Speaker Self-Esteem Needs, Speaker Self-Actualization Needs.

SPEAKER SECURITY NEEDS

Characteristics of fulfilling your Speaker Security Needs are: (1) feeling competent in the technical details of your topic, (2) feeling confident you can deliver your message to your audience, and (3) feeling confident you will be able to handle audience questions competently and confidently.

SPEAKER BELONGINGNESS NEEDS

Characteristics of fulfilling your Speaker Belongingness Needs are: (1) having several deep relationships with other speakers and clients, (2) belonging to speaker organizations like Toastmasters and the National Speakers Association, and (3) being accepted by the speaking organizations you belong to and engaged in stimulating conversations at meetings of these organizations.

SPEAKER SELF-ESTEEM NEEDS

Characteristics of fulfilling your Speaker Self-Esteem Needs are: (1) you feel respected for your speaking by members of your speaking organizations and others who have seen you speak, (2) you have attained status in your speaker organizations and other organizations you belong to where you have to speak frequently, and (3) you have received formal and informal recognition in your speaker organizations and other organizations you belong to where you have to speak frequently.

SPEAKER SELF-ACTUALIZATION NEEDS

Characteristics of fulfilling your Speaker Self-Actualization Needs are: (1) you feel you are approaching or have attained your full-potential as a speaker, (2) you are recognized nationally and internationally as the expert in your area of expertise, and (3) you have mastered your self-motivation and are an expert decision maker when it comes to speaking at any venue (e.g., keynotes, seminars, one-on-one/group coaching).

***

So where are you on your Speaker's Hierarchy of Needs for Security, Belongingness, Self-Esteem, and Self-Actualization?

Look at the Speaker's Hierarchy of Needs as a strategy you can use to become all you can be as a speaker!

CALL TO ACTION

- Identify where you are on your Speaker's Hierarchy of Needs.
- Develop planning objectives to satisfy your present need on the Speaker's Hierarchy of Needs.
- Develop action plans derived from your planning objectives to satisfy your present need on the Speaker's Hierarchy of Needs and move up to the next level.

"What is necessary to change a person is to change his awareness of himself."

—Abraham Maslow

"SO WHERE CAN I SPEAK?"

"Remember not only to say the right thing in the right place, but far more difficult still, to leave unsaid the wrong thing at the tempting moment."
—Benjamin Franklin

YOU KNOW YOU WANT to speak in public because you have something to say that can greatly benefit others. So where can you speak?

Organizations of all types are clamoring for speakers. They are looking to fill their programs for their daily/weekly/monthly meetings.

Below are some ideas on where you can speak.

SPEAK IN YOUR JOB POSITION

The inability of people not being able to get ahead abounds in the annals of human history. A large part of this is due to people not exploring opportunities right where they are. That's right! Before you go exploring speaking opportunities elsewhere, fully explore and exhaust the opportunities in your current job position.

There are a number of advantages you have in speaking in your current job position. Number one, people know you and you know the organization. Therefore, you know or have an idea as to who to contact for speaking opportunities. Number two, you probably have an advocate or two in your company that can give you a reference. Number three, you don't have to search outside your company where you may know no one. Though this is not impossible, it is many times harder to discover opportunities to speak when you look outside your company.

But let's say you still want to explore outside your company. Why not try to find speaking opportunities at colleges and universities?

SPEAK AT COLLEGES AND UNIVERSITIES

When adults go looking for training or education, they usually turn to their local college or university. Now, with the widespread use of distance learning, far away universities in which people will never visit are also possibilities for you to speak.

Your local and not-so-local colleges and universities are another avenue to explore for you to speak. Almost all colleges and universities have opportunities to teach regular classes in-person and online if you have expertise they need. A caveat, though: to teach a regular college/university class, you will need to have a graduate or doctorate degree.

However, colleges and universities also have continuing education short courses. If you have a needed expertise in a short course, say in public speaking, short courses may be available for you to teach.

SPEAK IN YOUR OWN BUSINESS

 This is the opportunity for which you might have been waiting. There are two types of speakers in their own business. There are those speakers who make their living solely by speaking. These are the keynote and seminar speakers. Then there are those who speak to market their business. There is also a hybrid business model that combines both.

In today's world, the hybrid business model is the most prevalent. There are speakers that may speak at conferences and other meetings. Chances are though they also coach clients in a myriad of areas from leadership to presentation skills to life coaching and many more.

**

Speaking in your current job position, at colleges and universities, or in your own business are by no means the only places you can speak. The basic formula is to determine what your particular expertise can offer others, determine your target market, and then show them how you can improve their lives. I know. Easier said than done, but possible.

So go forth and speak but remember when one door closes, another window opens. Keep the faith, maintain confidence in yourself, and you will discover opportunities to speak. It is a matter of when, not if!

CALL TO ACTION

- In the next week, explore speaking opportunities with your manager in your current position or in another position in your company.
- In the next week, call five colleges and universities to ask for the continuing education contact and then call this contact to discover what short-term speaking opportunities are available.
- Take inventory of your expertise, start taking notes on how your expertise can help others, and then talk to professional speakers to get advice on starting a speaking/ coaching business.

"Picture yourself in a living room having a chat with your friends. You would be relaxed and comfortable talking to them. The same applies when public speaking."

—Richard Branson

AS A SPEAKER, DO YOU HAVE AN ATTITUDE OF GRATITUDE?

"Thankfulness is the beginning of gratitude. Gratitude is the completion of thankfulness. Thankfulness may consist merely of words. Gratitude is shown in acts."
—Henri Frederic Amiel

DO YOU HAVE AN attitude of gratitude for the opportunities speaking before an in-person or virtual audience give you?

We will explore in this chapter your gratitude for the opportunities as a speaker to teach others, for self-expression, and to learn from others.

OPPORTUNITY TO TEACH OTHERS

 Do you have an attitude of gratitude for your opportunity to teach others?

Most of you are probably familiar with Stephen Covey's 1989 landmark book *The Seven Habits of Highly Effective People*.

You are probably less aware of a book he wrote in 1994 with A. Roger Merrill and Rebecca R. Merrill entitled *First Things First*. In this book, Covey and the Merrills tell us that all humans have the following needs: to live, to love, to learn, to leave a legacy. As a speaker, you have the opportunity to leave a legacy through your speaking, which gives you opportunities to teach others.

As you get older, it is natural for you to think about what you will leave our world. The recordings of your speeches and presentations, your writings, and your podcasts, to name a few legacies you will leave, will last for a very long time after you leave this earth. I often talk about Earl Nightingale as my mentor. I discovered his wonderfully instructive recordings in 1994, five years after he left our world. Those recordings taught me much about how to interact with others and also confirmed what I already knew.

Engender an attitude of gratitude for having the opportunity as a speaker to teach others. You will be leaving a legacy that will benefit many when you are alive and when you have passed from our world.

Your human need to live manifests itself in your self-expression.

OPPORTUNITY FOR SELF-EXPRESSION

 Do you have an attitude of gratitude for your opportunity for self-expression?

As a child, a teenager, and an adult, you wanted to be heard. You want to self-express your thoughts, beliefs, and viewpoints. Did you ever think why this is so? It is so because the very nature of human beings is to do so. We quite literally feel more alive when we express what is on our minds.

What a great opportunity we have as speakers to express ourselves. We maximize this opportunity when we keep our audiences in mind when we speak. Keeping the audience in mind as to what they need and want from your presentation will make you successful.

You may often think no one will want to listen to what you have to say when the direct opposite is true. Your audience has come to hear you speak. They want to know your thoughts on the topic of which you are speaking.

So engender an attitude of gratitude for having the opportunity as a speaker to self-express yourself for the benefit of others. You might be surprised how much others are eager to listen to what you have to say.

It is ironic, but your need to learn is satisfied even when you are teaching others. The old saying is true: "If you want to learn something, teach it." Teaching also affords you the opportunity to learn from others.

OPPORTUNITY TO LEARN FROM OTHERS

Do you have an attitude of gratitude for your opportunity to learn from others?

Why is the best method to learn something to teach it? You learn in the process of your detailed planning done way before you get up on the stage to deliver your presentation.

Your audience is forcing you to learn your topic before you even present to them. Winston Churchill would spend six to eight hours preparing a forty-minute speech. He spent *nine to twelve times* the duration of a forty-minute speech preparing for it. What does this tell you? If you want to deliver a great presentation, you have to put in the time preparing for it. This time provides you with a deep knowledge about your topic, whether you include it in your presentation or not. A by-product of this deep knowledge is you will be more confident when you deliver your presentation.

However, your learning does not stop when you have finished preparing your presentation. While you are delivering your presentation, questions and comments from your audience and new insights you get on the spot all add to your knowledge of your subject. The key to retaining this knowledge is to do what we called in the Air Force "hot wash." As soon as possible after your presentation, rerun your presentation through the "washer" of self-reflection and trusted friends' evaluations. Take written notes on what went great, what was "so-so," and what you will improve next time.

What an opportunity for you to learn!

***

In this chapter, we explored your gratitude for opportunities as a speaker to teach others, for self-expression, and to learn from others.

I will ask you again. Do you have an attitude of gratitude for your audience for the opportunities speaking before an in-person or virtual audience gives you?

You decide!

CALL TO ACTION

- Think of your presentations as a way to leave to the world a legacy of great speaking.
- Fully express yourself in your next presentation; people come to hear YOU speak.
- Learn from whatever role you are playing, speaker or audience member.

"Gratitude is not only the greatest of virtues but the parent of all others."

—Marcus Tullius Cicero

PART II: PRESENTATION PREPARATION (GENERAL)

PART I OF THIS book hopefully convinced you of the importance of great speaking in public. Now we turn to how you can you prepare yourself to speak greatly in public. Like anything else worth doing, there is a process for becoming a great speaker.

Bear Bryant, the legendary coach of the Alabama Crimson Tide football team said, "Everybody has the will to win, but few people have the will to prepare to win."

Part II of this book talks about the prerequisites to prepare to win in your presentations. It covers the following topics:

- "I've Been Asked to Speak. Now What?"
- Need a Presentation Quickly?
- Connect with Your Audience or Die!
- Make Your Presentations Compelling!
- Less Means More!
- Laser-Focus Your Presentation Purpose!

- "I Have My Speech Topic. Now What?"
- Great Presentations' Indispensable Ingredient!
- Adversity Reveals Great Speaking Tips!
- Your Presentation "Pain Points!"

"I'VE BEEN ASKED TO SPEAK. NOW WHAT?"

"If you can't communicate and talk to other people and get across your ideas, you're giving up your potential."
—Warren Buffet

YOU HAVE A CERTAIN expertise that other people want to know about and then it happens! You are asked to speak to your company's quarterly business meeting or at your industry's conference or, even worse, to your daughter's or son's eighth grade class. What do you do? Read on to find out.

FIND OUT ALL YOU CAN ABOUT YOUR AUDIENCE

In addition to being a speaker, I am also a practicing systems engineer. One of the tenets of systems engineering directly applicable to speaking is determining and managing the user's requirements. In the case of your audience, your job is to determine, to the best of your ability, your audience's expectations and meet and exceed those expectations.

As a U.S. Air Force officer, for part of my career, I helped develop electronic warfare subsystems for our jets to save pilots' lives. If I and my colleagues did not sufficiently develop and manage these electronic warfare subsystem requirements, it could literally mean a pilot could lose his or her life.

Now, I am not saying not knowing your audience is life threatening, but your presentation will be a lot more successful if you find out what your audience expects to hear, satisfy these expectations, and exceed them.

How do you do this? There are a myriad of ways. A few follow:

- Talk to the person who asked you to speak before your presentation. Odds are, they are a member of the organization to whom you will speak. This person will have very pertinent information about your audience. Ask them questions like, "What are the demographics of your audience?" "What are the 'pain points' of audience members?" and "What is the ideal maximum time for which this audience likes to hear a talk?" There are a number of other questions you can ask. You know them. Ask them.

- Ask permission to contact a few people in your audience well prior to your presentation. Call or e-mail these audience members. Ask them how much they know about your subject. Ask them their opinion on your topic. Ask them what they would like to learn about your topic. The questions are almost endless.

- Review organization publications. Listen to organization podcasts and view organization videos if these are available. These information outlets usually reflect what your audience is interested in and will give you are good idea as to what their opinions are on your subject.

- Review talks this audience has experienced before. Ask the person who asked you to talk how these previous topics were received. Find out why they were hits or "bombs."

***

So you have discovered your audience's expectations for your presentation and are designing your presentation to satisfy and exceed these expectations. But do you have the time to develop a completely new presentation? Of course not. There is a solution to this: reuse prior presentation material.

REUSE SPEAKING MATERIAL FROM ONE OF YOUR PRIOR PRESENTATIONS?

Life is short. There is not enough time in your life to develop a completely new presentation every time you are asked to speak. One of the tenets of object-oriented programming is reuse. This type of reuse helps to lower the cost of software, reduce software programming "bugs," and speed up the programming process. This is done by breaking down the task into subtask modules that the programmer can fit together to complete the current task.

The same principle can be applied to your speaking. Modularize your speaking so you can mix and match modules to produce the first draft of your next presentation in a fraction of the time you would need to produce a completely new presentation. Your time is money. Doing things in less time saves you for other important tasks. It also reduces errors in your presentation because you have already developed the presentation modules before.

Do you have a similar presentation, although not exactly the same topic, in which you can reuse its material? If the topic of your upcoming presentation is Leadership in the Workplace, can you use material from your presentation entitled "Leadership is Learned, Not Inherited?" If you have a workshop for adults covering goalsetting, can you adapt this to your next presentation teaching goalsetting to high schoolers? If you have a talk teaching presentation skills to an HR audience, can you use the same material in showing the dos and don'ts of public speaking to university professors?

See what I mean about reuse? You may tend to recreate what you have already created before. Resist the urge. Your time will be better spent practicing your presentation.

You have discovered your audience's expectations for your presentation and have discovered the joys of reusing material from your prior presentations.

Even with knowing your audience's expectations and reusing prior presentation material, there will still be gaps in your presentation. What do you do? Everyone has heard of brainstorming, and the application of this group technique is great if you have access to other people. Let's suppose you don't. Mind storming is the answer. Although not as effective as brainstorming, mind storming can be a great help when it is eleven p.m., you have your presentation tomorrow, and you are alone.

MIND STORM AND DEVELOP TOPICS RELEVANT TO YOUR AUDIENCE'S DESIRES

Mind storming comes from Brian Tracy's Ultimate Goals program; the premise is that you state your goal in the form of a question then "mind storm" twenty answers to that question. If you are hunting for ideas for your presentation, this is a great way by yourself to get those golden idea nuggets. From "Mind Storming with Brian Tracy" (https://paulguyon.com/629/mind-storming-with-brian-tracy/) follow the below steps:

1. Take out a pen and a blank sheet of paper. Use paper instead of a computer. There is something special about handwriting your answers out with a pen or pencil. It helps to make connections in your brain that would otherwise not form.

2. Write your top goal in the form of a question at the top of the page. Your question should be specific and time bound, for example, "How can I double my income to $100,000 per year by December 31, 2012?"

3. Then write out exactly twenty answers to the question.

4. Do not judge your answers. Do not put any thought as to how practical or possible an answer is. That part comes later. We are trying to get as many ideas on paper to consider later.

5. Your first five to ten answers will be easy, like work harder, longer, sell more stuff, etc.

6. As you press on, the next ten answers will be much more difficult. This is where the magic happens. Keep going.

7. Once you have twenty answers, then and only then qualify them.

8. Optionally, choose the best answer and form it into a question and repeat the process again.

9. Choose the best answer and get to work on it right away.

10. "Rinse" and repeat the process often.

Use these ideas again with your audience's expectations in mind. If you do, the problem you will have is sifting through all the great ideas you discover, not despairing because you have no ideas.

***

So, when you are asked to speak, don't fret. If you discover your audience's expectations, reuse material from your prior presentations, and use mind storming to fill in the gaps in your presentation, you are well on your way to delivering a dynamic, relevant, and interesting presentation. Who knows? Your audience might even give you a standing ovation!

CALL TO ACTION

- Find out all you can about your audience before your presentation (e.g., demographics, what they know about your subject, are they for or against your subject and why, etc.).
- Don't create new material for each presentation. Use previously created material to the greatest extent.
- Mind storm (Mind Storming with Brian Tracy) (www.paulguyon.com/629/mind-storming-with-brian-tracy/) to develop your topic.

"Speakers who talk about what life has taught them never fail to keep the attention of their listeners."

—Dale Carnegie

NEED A PRESENTATION QUICKLY?

"All great speakers were bad speakers at first."
—Ralph Waldo Emerson

IT IS THE DAY before your big speech and you are not nearly done developing it and practicing it. What can you do?

Learn how to uncover and organize your ideas quickly, make it simple for yourself and your audience by using three main points, and craft great openings and closings fast.

USE MIND MAPPING TO UNCOVER AND ORGANIZE IDEAS QUICKLY

You may be a linear thinker and don't need to see how your ideas fit together, but there are a whole lot of us that can generate more ideas visually more quickly than we can linearly. Consider using mind mapping to generate ideas faster. So what is mind mapping?

According to Mindmapping.com (www.mindmapping.com), mind mapping is a highly effective way of getting information in and out of your brain. Mind mapping is a creative and logical means of notetaking and note making that literally "maps out" your ideas.

All mind maps have some things in common. They have a natural organizational structure that radiates from the center and use lines, symbols, words, color, and images according to simple, brain-friendly concepts. Mind mapping converts a long list of monotonous information into a colorful, memorable, and highly organized diagram that works in line with your brain's natural way of doing things.

The Five Essential Characteristics of Mind Mapping are:

1. The main idea, subject, or focus is crystallized in a central image.
2. The main themes radiate from the central image as "branches."
3. The branches comprise a key image or key word drawn or printed on its associated line.

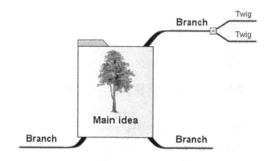

4. Topics of lesser importance are represented as "twigs" of the relevant branch.
5. The branches form a connected nodal structure.

HOW TO MAKE A MIND MAP

1. Think of your general main theme and write it down in the center of the page, e.g., food.
2. Figure out sub-themes of your main concept and draw branches to them from the center, beginning to look like a spider web, e.g., meats, dairy, breads.
3. Make sure to use very short phrases or even single words.
4. Add images to invoke thought or get the message across better.

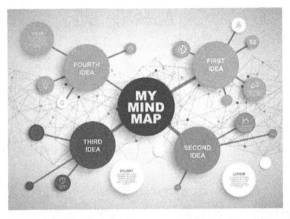

5. Try to think of at least two main points for each sub-theme you created and create branches out to those.

USE THREE MAIN POINTS ALWAYS

From Potent Speaking (www.potentspeaking.com/3-points/) on why you should use three main points in your presentation:

It is simpler for the audience. Modern audiences are not easy to keep engaged. With a low attention span and a general disinterest in most speeches, you've got to do all you can do make your speech easy to digest. In most contexts, people won't be writing down your points. It's hard for people to remember more than three main points, especially if you don't have much time to spend on them.

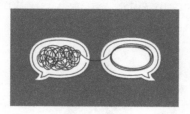

Your points are usually not as clear as you think. People who use too many points often have to speed through their speech in order to fit everything. This means the audience usually won't be able to digest your points or get a full understanding of them. Speechwriters have already studied the subject for a while before they start writing their speech. By that time, they are pretty familiar with it. As a result, they usually do not have an accurate view of how to explain it to someone else. I call this problem prior knowledge bias: when you think you explained something well because you already get it, but other people are just confused.

It's easy to go over time. When you have more than three points, it becomes harder to keep track of time and apportion it properly. You'll often end up rushing the last couple of points or going over time. There are few things worse than going longer than your allotted time. It's disrespectful to the audience.

Think about it: all those people in the crowd are actually there to hear you speak. They have agreed to sit down quietly and listen to what you have to say for a set period of time. Going over time is like buying super expensive food because someone else is picking up the tab.

It helps you to do deeper analysis. If you spend more time on each point, you can develop them better. Give more reasons why they are true, or read more quotes, or show more PowerPoint images. You will have more success trying to convince the audience of one to three things with deep analysis than convincing them of four or more points with shallow analysis.

It helps you avoid weak points. When you try to include too many points in your speech, you'll often end up including points that are not particularly persuasive or helpful. This is a matter of quantity over quality.

HAVE A GREAT OPENING AND CLOSING

There have been a multitude of studies performed about what audience members remember from presentations. The results are in. Audience members remember beginnings and endings. So, what does this tell you? Your presentation openings and closings have to be memorable to make your presentation memorable. Some ways you can you do this are:

 Stories: Everyone loves a good story. Before there were iPhones, Snapchat, television, newspapers, radio, there were stories. I am sure you have seen prehistoric etchings on the walls of caves. Those etchings tell a story and enthralled the audience at the time.

A GOAL WITHOUT
A PLAN IS
JUST A WISH

Quotes: Quotes are powerful because they make us take a mental break and think. My favorite quotes are those from world leaders throughout the ages: George Washington, Abraham Lincoln, and Winston Churchill, to name a few. Don't know any famous relevant quotes? Google the word "quotes" and the subject of the quotes, and you will get more quotes than you can possibly use.

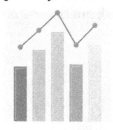 **Statistics:** Statistics can immediately change how people think about things. For instance, most people think suicide rates actually skyrocket around Christmastime. In reality, the Center for Disease Control (CDC) actually reports that suicide rates are actually lowest in December. The suicide rate actually peaks in the spring, not the winter. Statistics are powerful. Make sure they are relevant to your presentation.

Humor: Earl Nightingale said, "The only requirement for a speaker is to be interesting." Laughing actually opens yours and your audience's minds because when we laugh, we will be open to more ideas from others. The author Norman Cousins actually helped cure himself of a terrible sickness by watching videotapes of comedian teams like the Three Stooges, Laurel and Hardy, and Abbott and Costello.

Rhetorical Questions: Rhetorical questions, of course, are questions not meant to be answered by your audience. They are questions that provoke thought such as, "Have you ever thought about how your heritage affects your point of view?" or "What should be humanity's goal?" or "If you could teach the entire world just one concept, what would it be?" These questions open the minds of your audience and provide you with multiple paths in which to take your presentation.

Share your story

A Personal Experience: Audiences love to hear about your personal experiences. It makes you human and approachable. A personal foible of yours will be particularly loved by your audience. Experiment and don't be afraid to poke fun at yourself. The rewards from this are plenty.

***

On the day before your big speech, don't fret. Rev up your engine, uncover and organize your ideas quickly using mind mapping, make it simple for yourself and your audience by sticking to three main points, and craft great openings and closings fast by using stories, quotes, statistics, humor, rhetorical questions, or a personal experience.

You'll be glad you did and have a "knock your socks off" presentation.

CALL TO ACTION

- Use mind mapping (Mindmapping.com) to develop and organize ideas quickly.
- Always use three main points for your presentations because they are easily remembered by your audience.
- Have great openings and closings because people remember beginnings and endings.

"The right word may be effective, but no word was ever as effective as a rightly timed pause."

—Mark Twain

CONNECT WITH YOUR AUDIENCE OR DIE!

"Remember not only to say the right thing in the right place, but far more difficult still, to leave unsaid the wrong thing at the tempting moment."

—Benjamin Franklin

DO YOU WANT YOUR audiences to take what you say in your presentations and apply it in their own lives? Of course you do. What other reward is there for a speaker?

In this chapter, we will examine three great ways to connect with your audience: (1) have a conversation with your audience, (2) interpret and react to your audience's body language, and (3) tell stories to your audience.

HAVE A CONVERSATION WITH YOUR AUDIENCE

Do you listen more attentively to someone you like or someone you don't like? If you are like me, you will be much more inclined to listen to the person you like. It is the same way in your presentations.

Giving a presentation is very similar to having a conversation with a single person. So, when you are presenting, imagine yourself having a conversation with a single person in your audience. What are some of the things you would do?

For one, you would look the other person in the eye. There is nothing more annoying than talking to someone while they are not looking at you. What is the first thing you think of when this happens? Of course. The other person is not listening to you. Good eye contact says a number of things. It says, "You are important to me." It says, "I value you and what you are saying." It says, "I respect you."

Another thing you do during a conversation is you clarify what the other person is saying. You say things like, "Let me tell you what I think you are saying. Please correct me if I am wrong." Another frustration people have when you are talking to them is being misinterpreted. People want to know your meaning of what they are saying is what they intended. So, ask your audience occasionally whether they are getting the meaning of what you are saying.

Now think about your presentations and how you can use the methods of a one-on-one conversation to connect with your audience. Certainly, good eye contact is essential. It tells your audience you are interested in them.

Although you normally do not get verbal feedback during your presentation, try to anticipate how your audience can misinterpret what you are saying. Say the same thing in a different way and then watch their body language. Think about how words in your presentation might not have the same exact meaning in the venue region. For instance, in the Midwest, a danish is called a sweet roll.

Having a conversation with your audience will better connect you to them. Becoming an expert at reading your audience's body language and how to react to it "on the fly" will put you in an elite group of speakers.

INTERPRET AND REACT TO YOUR AUDIENCE'S BODY LANGUAGE

Being able to read your audience's body language is absolutely essential to connecting with your audience. As in one-on-one conversation, whenever body language does not match the words the other person is saying, the body language will always betray how the other person is really feeling.

The following is from "How to Read Body Language — 5 Ways Your Audience Can Make You a Better Speaker" (www.genardmethod.com/blog/how-to-read-body-language-5-ways-your-audience-can-make-you-a-better-speaker) concerning how to read audience body language:

- ***Pay attention to your audience's mood***. As speakers, we can't make the mistake of wearing a blindfold when we present, determined at all costs to deliver the presentation we came to give! Your audience, moment by moment, is sending out signals you need to be observing if you're going to continue to connect with them and meet them where they live. Of course, you should do your best to understand your audience ahead of time.

- ***Does everyone start taking notes?*** Just as important as negative visual feedback, are the instances where listeners show you that what you're saying is valuable to them. Clearly, one of those times is when the pens, pads, and styluses emerge. Did you just say something that listeners suddenly think is important enough to write down? It's actually one of the more dramatic ways your audience gives you a vote of confidence. Interestingly enough, most of the time this happens, I've found, it's a universal effect: at the same time, everybody feels the need to memorialize what you just said.

- ***Heads up? Nodding? They're giving you clues.*** If audience members are looking at you brightly and nodding enthusiastically, you should feel a warm glow. The head nod doesn't just indicate that people are suddenly paying attention. It is actually showing acceptance of the point you've just been making. This is much more than a clue that you should use this material again. It's also giving you insight into the thinking of these listeners.

- ***Facial Expressions and What They are Telling You***. We humans depend to an extraordinary extent on facial expressions to be able to successfully interact with others of our species. Trustworthiness? Motive? Affection or aversion? Comprehension or confusion? Impatience? Anger? Happiness? Engagement? Fascination?
  - We see, and process, all of these responses and many, many more through the facial expressions of the people we're speaking to. This aspect of body language is a powerful and reliable tool for understanding and connecting with the people we interact with every day of our lives.

- **<u>Body of Evidence. Posture and Movement.</u>** We all tend to make ourselves comfortable when we're settling in to hear a pitch, a presentation, or extended remarks. Keep this fact in mind when you notice audience members sitting back or wearing a placid expression. Not everyone will be nodding delightedly at what you say. (And you must avoid playing to those listeners exclusively!)
  - How significant is it, then, when they sit up and lean forward, cast a glance with raised eyebrow at fellow audience members, or move closer to the screen displaying your slide deck? The answer is that these changes in posture or movement are significant indeed. Every actress knows when she has an audience in the palm of her hand. Be sure to pay attention if it's just happened in your presentation! You're now in territory you should explore further, perhaps even asking the audience a question or giving them some other invitation to participate.

Having a conversation and reading your audience's body language will greatly help you to connect with your audience.

The third and final way to connect with your audience is to tell relevant stories.

USE STORIES TO CONNECT

Who doesn't love a story? Before man had the ability to record what was happening, stories were used to pass history on from generation to generation. If you are not telling relevant stories to your audience, you are missing a great opportunity to connect with them.

From the "Importance of Stories" (https://lumen.instructure. com/courses/218897/pages/linkedtext54220?module_item_ id=5007073) :

Storytelling is a crucial component to effective public speaking. It creates relevance for the audience, providing additional detail and mental visuals that bring to life otherwise dull, remote, or complex topics.

Stories give speakers the opportunity to tell personal stories that relate to the audiences' experiences, thought processes, or values. Moreover, including stories in both interpersonal communication and public speaking helps your audience remember your statements or speech for later recall.

According to Chip and Dan Heath, authors of *Made to Stick*, telling stories is one of the most important things that public speakers can do to make their presentations memorable. This is perhaps due to storytelling's role as one of the few human traits that is truly universal regardless of age, gender, culture, and language.

Stories help us connect with our audiences in a way that charts, graphs, statistics, and bullet points cannot. They help us make our messages stick and our speeches memorable.

So stories are essential to making your presentation main points stick with your audience. Don't leave home without them!

***

To connect with your audience, have a conversation with them, read and react to their body language, and tell lots of stories.

If you do these things, you will find your audience more attentive, more interested in what you are saying, and most importantly, they will apply what you say in their lives. Isn't that the whole point of speaking?

CALL TO ACTION

- Deliver your presentation as you would a conversation with another person.
- Use your audience's body language cues to readjust your presentation delivery on the fly.
- Use stories, preferably personal stories, to connect with your audience.

"Listen with curiosity. Speak with honesty. Act with integrity."

—Roy Bennett

MAKE YOUR PRESENTATIONS COMPELLING!

"No one can remember more than three points."
—Phillip Crosby

ON THE AFTERNOON OF Thursday, November 19, 1863, there were two people who spoke on the Gettysburg battlefield. The first speaker was eloquent and spoke for two hours. The second speaker was also eloquent, but only spoke 283 words, which have been remembered ever since as the Gettysburg Address delivered by President Abraham Lincoln. Do you remember who the first speaker was? The first speaker was then famed orator and former Secretary of State Edward Everett. Who do you think was more interesting and memorable to the audience that day?

One of my mentors, the radio personality Earl Nightingale, said, "The only obligation of a speaker is to make their presentation interesting for his or her audience." So how do we make our presentations interesting?

PRESENT MINIMUM INFORMATION TO YOUR AUDIENCE

The first way, believe it or not, is to present to your audience the minimum information they need to understand your main points. Less is more emphatic!

I listened to a colleague's presentation once. Her presentation had too much detail. The presentation should have taken fifteen to twenty minutes. It grew into an hour-long presentation and would have gone longer if someone else didn't have the meeting room booked after us. She had unnecessary detail that not only lengthened her presentation but also muddled her main points. Her audience was baffled as to what her main points were.

Lost audiences are tuned-out audiences. Too many details in your presentation distract the audience from your main points. As a technical speaker, I have experienced this both on the presenting and receiving ends.

There is also another unexpected danger when you include unnecessary details. Audience members invariably ask questions about the unnecessary details and your presentation goes in directions you had not intended, wasting time, diluting your main points, and making your presentation less interesting.

Abraham Lincoln adroitly illustrated a saying in public speaking circles, "Be bold, be brief, be gone!" Say what you have come to say in a dynamic and concise manner and then sit down. Don't fall in love with the sound of your voice!

TELL STORIES THAT SUPPORT YOUR MAIN POINTS

The second way to make your presentations interesting is to tell stories that support your main points. Everyone loves a story, and we all have stories. You may not think you do, but you do. Think back to that presentation you liked or didn't like or the situation in the lunchroom that is relevant to your presentation. Tell an historical story about your subject area. Self-deprecating stories are particularly loved by audiences drawing them to you and your topic. Here's the key rule about stories: the story must be relevant to the point you are making at the time.

VARY YOUR PRESENTATION METHOD

 Finally, the third way to make your presentations more interesting is to vary your presentation method. The average adult's attention span is twenty minutes. At least every twenty minutes, change your presentation method. Ask the audience questions to get them involved. Show a video. Pass around a prop relevant to the subject. Bringing variety to your presentations will make them more interesting for your audience and for yourself.

Do you want your presentations to be interesting for your audiences? Sure, you do.

Remember, you can make your presentation more interesting, i.e., less boring, by:

- One: Giving your audience the minimum they need to understand your point.
- Two: Telling stories. Everyone loves a story.
- Three: Varying your presentation method (e.g., Ask the audience questions, show videos, pass out props, etc.)

Take these three speaking tips to heart, make them a part of your presentation, and you will find your audiences saying, "Now that was a great presentation."

CALL TO ACTION

- Give your audience the minimum amount of information they need to understand your main points.
- Tell stories, preferably personal stories, to illustrate your main points.
- Vary your presentation methods (e.g., show a video, pass around a prop, ask your audience questions, etc.)

"The brain doesn't pay attention to boring things."

—John Medina

LESS MEANS MORE!

"Brevity is the best recommendation of speech, whether in a senator or an orator."

—Marcus Tullius Cicero

HAVE YOU EVER TALKED to a friend, colleague, or your boss and were wondering during the conversation, "What is his/her main point?" I know I have. If you are not careful, the same thing could happen during your presentations.

This chapter delves into why shorter presentations keep your audience engaged with you and are easier for your audience to follow and what advantages they bring to you as a speaker.

SHORTER PRESENTATIONS KEEP YOUR AUDIENCE ENGAGED

As I brought up in the previous chapter, when Abraham Lincoln recited the Gettysburg Address, he was able to keep his audience engaged because he said what he had to say in a short amount of words. When you say the fewest words possible in your presentations, your audience will be interested in your speech, and it will be memorable to them.

There is a saying in public speaking circles: "Be bold, be brief, be gone." Your interesting presentation gets less interesting as time goes on. Don't fall in love with the sound of your voice.

I recently heard a speaker drone on for twenty-eight minutes where other speakers of the same subject usually speak for ten to fifteen minutes. How do I know it was twenty-eight minutes? I kept an eye on my watch. I had heard this speaker before and knew he was long-winded. The main problem with long presentations is they confuse the audience. Long presentations tend to have spots where the audience thinks the speaker is concluding. When the speaker does not end, the audience wonders where the speaker will end. This causes your audience to disengage. Don't let this happen with your presentations.

So shorter presentations keep your audience engaged. It also makes your presentations easier to follow.

SHORTER PRESENTATIONS ARE EASIER TO FOLLOW FOR YOUR AUDIENCE

 Toastmasters tells us whether your presentation is ten minutes, one hour, or three hours, have only three main points. Why is this? This is because your audience can easily remember the three main points of your presentation. It is as simple as that.

Think of famous speeches from history and how long they were.

- George Washington—2nd Inaugural Address (1793), 135 words (founders.archives.gov/documents/Washington/05-12-02-0200)
- Martin Luther King—"I Have a Dream" speech (1963), 17 minutes (https://www.btboces.org/Downloads/I%20Have%20a%20Dream%20by%20Martin%20Luther%20King%20Jr.pdf)
- Neil Armstrong—"That's one small step for man, one giant leap for mankind" (1969), 12 words

Read the above speeches and you will find them easy to follow mostly because of their brevity. Every word was painstakingly crafted to "pull its weight" and directly contribute to the speaker's main points.

Remember, you should only have three points in your speech. After every point, review the previous points. This will make it easier for your audience to follow your logic. It will also help your audience see how each main point builds on the previous main point.

So shorter presentations keep your audience engaged and make your presentation easier to follow. But what advantages do they give you, the speaker?

SHORTER PRESENTATIONS PROVIDE ADVANTAGES TO THE SPEAKER

Shorter presentations are easier to present because there is less material to remember to present. Put together a set of bullet points that are your main points supported by sub-bullet points.

 Because shorter presentations are easier to present, they give you time to truly craft how you want to say the words in your presentation. Always speak ideas and not words. Wean yourself off of the actual words on paper.

Because your presentation is short, you will not get confused by the different parts of your presentation. Memorize the ideas of your presentation's three main points and their sub-points (three sub-points per main point). Speak ideas, not words.

Because your presentation is shorter, your visuals can be simpler and easier to follow for your audience. Use images liberally on your visuals. Limit the text as much as you can or even eliminate the text on your visuals altogether, if possible. The amount of attention your audience gives to you and your message is inversely proportionate to the amount of text you have on your visuals. The more text on your visuals, the less the audience will be listening to you. So decrease the text on your visuals and increase the impact of your presentation.

***

So what have we covered in this chapter? Shorter presentations keep your audience engaged and make it easier for the audience to follow your main points—and, therefore, increase your presentation's impact. Finally, shorter presentations provide the speaker with distinct advantages over longer presentations.

If you make your points in a shorter presentation, it will have more impact. Who wouldn't want that?

CALL TO ACTION

- Keep your presentations short to keep your audience's attention.
- Keep your presentations short so it is easier for you to remember and present.
- Use images on your slides as much as possible; reduce words on your slides as much as possible.

"In making a speech one must study three points: first, the means of producing persuasion; second, the language; third, the proper arrangement of the various parts of the speech."

—Aristotle

LASER-FOCUS YOUR PRESENTATION PURPOSE!

"Don't wish it was easier, wish you were better. Don't wish for less problems, wish for more skills. Don't wish for less challenge, wish for more wisdom."

—Jim Rohn

THE FIRST BOOK I bought when I became interested in public speaking a number of decades ago was *Power Speak* by Dorothy Leeds. The book, which is still in print, covers all facets of public speaking, from overcoming the six major speaking faults to conquering trouble spots in your presentations to mastering the fine points of powerful speaking. Make sure it is on your bookshelf. Read it.

In this chapter, I will cover how to overcome one of the six major speaking faults to covering trouble spots: Unclear Purpose from *Power Speak*. What follows is (1) how to determine your presentation purpose, (2) the six main purposes of presentations, and (3) not letting your subject get too broad.

What follows is from *Power Speak*. I may move around some of the words, but the essential information is from this book.

HOW TO DETERMINE YOUR PURPOSE

 When you are establishing the purpose of your presentation, always start with the audience in mind. Begin by asking two questions: "What do I want to accomplish in the minds of those in my audience? What do I want them to do, feel, or know?"

Knowing clearly how you want the members of your audience to feel will affect the mood of your presentation, your choice of examples and stories, and how you build your argument. Every element is influenced by the effect of your overall purpose.

It can be surprisingly tough to set down a clear-cut statement of your purpose. The confusion of what your purpose is can stem from you attempting to convey too much to make sure your audience gets all the facts. If your presentation is overloaded with facts, you may not be able to get back to your original message.

Your presentation's purpose should be so clear that no one is left in doubt as to what your purpose is. When your purpose is defined at the outset, you can make sure all that follows supports your aims and that no one ends up wondering what point you were trying to get across.

Determining the purpose of your presentation is the first step. Did you know there are six main purposes of presentations? Here they are:

SIX MAIN PURPOSES OF PRESENTATIONS

Most presentations fit into one of the six categories in the list that follows. Each requires a different tone, different types of stories, different examples, even a different choice of words.

- ***To Inform.*** When the purpose of your presentation is to inform, you are simply attempting to convey information that your audience needs. The information might be the new promotion system for your company or the reorganization of your customer or even the chances the next asteroid will hit the earth. This kind of speech is usually fairly short and to the point and concentrates on the facts of the situation.

- ***To Instruct.*** When the purpose of your presentation is to instruct, you are still conveying information to your audience, but you are also teaching them to take action in some way. This action could be to teach them how to fill out the forms for the company's new insurance policy, how to use the company's new time charging system, or how to use the company's current airline reservation system. The point is not only are you conveying information, but you are also teaching your audience to take action.

- ***To Entertain.*** Unless you are a real entertainer, you probably will not make presentations solely to entertain. However, you can always deliver your presentation in an entertaining way. Audiences that are entertained enjoy your presentation more, retain more of your presentation, and most importantly, take action on the information in your presentation.

- **To Inspire/Motivate.** There are many ways to inspire and motivate people. Some people talk about a hardship they have overcome like cancer remission, the death of a spouse, or a debilitating physical challenge. However, motivating presentations do not solely concentrate on hardship. Martin Luther King inspired us to "be judged by the content of our character and not the color of our skin." Susan B. Anthony inspired millions to fight for women's right to vote. Abraham Lincoln inspired us in his second inaugural address to have "malice toward none."

- **To Activate/Stimulate.** The purpose of your presentation could be to activate or stimulate your audience to take an action. The specific purpose of your presentation could be to stimulate your audience to donate to a worthy cause. It could also be to activate your company's employees to "go the extra mile" with their customers. It could also be to vote for a referendum on the ballot.

- **To Persuade.** If the purpose of your presentation is to persuade, you would be using logic, evidence, and emotion to align your audience with your position. Some examples of this purpose are to persuade your audience to vote for your candidate, attend a town council meeting considering relaxing criminal sentencing laws, or to periodically join their neighbors to clean up ponds and streams in the local area.

You now know how to determine your presentation's purpose and the six purpose categories. Let's now look at why you shouldn't let your presentation subject get too broad.

DON'T LET YOUR SUBJECT GET TOO BROAD

When the purpose gets too broad, it gets confused with the subject. Keep these two separate and you're well on your way to focusing your presentation. You may be asked to speak on "Weapons of War in the Twentieth Century." A topic like this is just a broad subject; your purpose is to make a specific point about twentieth-century weapons—maybe even a specific weapon system category—through examples, anecdotes, and various facts. So tackle some key "trees," not the whole "forest."

The more focused and specific your presentation, the better your chances some words will resonate. Speak vividly about the leadership of one person, and your audience can glean much about leadership in general. Let people make the leap from the specific to the general, while you continue to be vivid. Broad subjects can become wonderful presentations if you give them a narrow and, therefore, memorable purpose and focus.

***

So you have learned how to determine the purpose of your presentation, the six main purposes of your presentations, and how to limit your subject to a manageable size.

Clear purpose in your presentations is an absolute must if you want your audience to get the full impact of your presentation.

If you don't have a clear purpose, you will be like Alice asking the Cheshire Cat which fork in the road she should take when she does not know where she wants to go.

Don't be like Alice!

CALL TO ACTION

- To determine your presentation's purpose, start with your audience.
- Select one of the standard purposes of a presentation (i.e., to inform, to instruct, to entertain, to inspire/motivate, to activate/simulate, to persuade).
- Don't let your subject get too broad.

*"Make sure that you have finished
speaking before your audience has finished listening!"*

—Dorothy Sarnoff

"I HAVE MY SPEECH TOPIC. NOW WHAT?"

"Let thy speech be better than silence, or be silent."
—Dionysius of Halicarnassus

OLD DIONYSIUS HAD IT right. So let's get right to how to make your speech better than silence.

You have your speech topic assigned from your boss, teacher, or yourself. Now what? You are probably thinking, "So how do I put this speech together?"

Begin with the body of your talk, then develop your opening and closing. The reason for this is your opening and closing are directly dependent on the body of your talk.

Below are three steps I have found useful to develop my talks from only starting with the topic:

STEP 1: MIND STORM (BRAINSTORMING ALONE) ALL IDEAS PERTAINING TO YOUR TOPIC

In this step, you want to generate as many ideas as possible about your topic. This is called Mind Storming. Mind storming is similar to brainstorming, only idea generation is not in a group. It is strictly done by you.

A major roadblock to brainstorming and mind storming is evaluating ideas as they are being generated. As you generate these ideas about your topic, you must resist the urge to evaluate the ideas. Remember, you want to generate as many ideas as possible about your topic. Evaluating these ideas as you are generating them actually stops the generation process.

Assuming you can resist the urge to evaluate your ideas, in two minutes generate as many ideas as possible. Some of your ideas will seem silly. Some will seem not even on the subject. Some will be "spot on" for your topic. Why two minutes? It's ironic, but when you feel the pressure of time, your ideas will flow more easily. If you feel after two minutes that all your ideas on your topic have not been discovered, take another two minutes, but no more.

When you have finished your idea generation period, use the Cards on the Wall method to group your ideas into like categories. Remember, in the Cards on the Wall exercise, you put each topic idea you generated on a separate Post-it note ("yellow sticky") and then logically group them on a board. After all your ideas are on the board, you will magically start seeing patterns of your ideas emerging. These patterns become the main points of your speech.

If possible, strive to winnow the Cards on the Wall to three groups. Three groups or main points is enough to make your talk interesting for the audience without having them remember too many main points. Three main points have the added benefit that it will be easier for you to remember only three main points.

After you have these three main points, use the ideas in each group to support the one main point.

So you have the body of your speech developed. Now, let us discuss the "bookends of your speech"—the opening and closing.

STEP 2: DEVELOP YOUR OPENING BY CAPTURING YOUR AUDIENCE'S ATTENTION

You may think in the opening to your speeches the only thing you have to do is tell the audience what you are going to tell them. However, the purpose of your speech opening is really to capture the audience's attention, focus them on your main points, and influence them to be eager to hear the details of your main points. There are several ways to do this. Some of these ways are:

Start your speech with a quote. For instance, if your speech is about the startling pace of technology, you could state the following:

> "Naveen Jain said, 'We are now living in a fast-paced technological era where every skill that we teach our children becomes obsolete in ten to fifteen years due to exponentially growing technological advances.' How can we ever expect our children to keep up?"

Start your speech with a story. You can tell an inspiring story about yourself or someone in history such as:

> *"I pride myself on my persistence as an engineer to determine the right solution to an engineering problem. My upbringing gave me that. I remember a situation when I was ten years old and what it taught me about the great benefits of persistence. I was sitting in the kitchen of my home and. . ."*

Start your speech with a startling statistic. For instance, if your topic is on the advances in computing power over the last fifty years, you can say, holding up your iPhone:

> *"The latest phones typically have 4GB of RAM. That is 34,359,738,368 bits. This is more than one million (1,048,576 to be exact) times more memory than the Apollo 11 guidance computer had in RAM. The iPhone also has up to 512GB of ROM memory. That is 4,398,046,511,104 bits, which is more seven million times more than that of the Apollo 11 guidance computer." (from* "Your Mobile Phone vs. Apollo 11's Guidance Computer") *(https://www.realclearscience. com/articles/2019/07/02/your_mobile_phone_vs_ apollo_11s_guidance_computer_111026.html)*

In other words, you want to capture the audience's attention in an interesting way. In addition to capturing the audience's attention, briefly state the three main points of your speech.

Quotes, stories, and startling statistics are not the only ways you can capture your audience's attention. Pick up any book on public speaking and you will find a list of other ways to add impact to your speech openings. These ways to add impact to your speech work for either openings or closings. The next section covers three more appropriate for both.

Remember, above all, whatever you use to create impact must be relevant to your topic.

So you have the body of your speech and your speech opening. The final step in developing your speech topic is to develop the closing.

STEP 3: DEVELOP YOUR CLOSING BY REVIEWING YOUR MAIN POINTS AND GIVING YOUR AUDIENCE A CALL TO ACTION

Audiences remember what you say at the beginning and the end of your speeches more than the body. So the closing of your speech, in addition to reviewing your main points briefly, must leave the audience with a lasting favorable impression of your speech. How do you do this?

You can add impact to your closings by using devices I mentioned in step two—quotes, stories, startling statistics. In addition, you can use humor, a poem, or make a relevant referral to a well-known movie. This is not an all-inclusive list. Google "ways to close a speech" and you will find many more.

One last thing: It is always good to include a call to action for your audience. In other words, what do you want your audience to do after the speech to implement what you said in the speech? This always plays well with an audience because they feel the return on the investment of their time is increased by changing something positively in their personal or professional lives.

***

I have not mentioned it yet in this chapter, but continually practicing your speech is essential to you becoming comfortable speaking to an audience.

When you are stumped as to what to do next once you have your topic, do the following: (1) mind storm all ideas pertaining to your topic, (2) develop your opening by capturing your audience's attention, and (3) develop your closing by reviewing your main points and giving your audience a call to action.

Follow these three steps and you will be amazed at how they help you develop your topic quickly, and maybe, just maybe, you will find yourself enjoying the process!

CALL TO ACTION

- Use mind storming to create ideas pertaining to your topic.
- Use quotes, stories, or startling statistics in your presentation opening to capture and keep your audience's attention.
- For your presentation closing, review your main points briefly, give your audience a call to action, and then, like the opening, end with a quote, relevant story, or startling statistic.

"Ninety percent of how well the talk will go is determined before the speaker steps on the platform."

—Somers White

GREAT PRESENTATIONS' INDISPENSABLE INGREDIENT!

"Your smile is your logo, your personality is your business card, how you leave others feeling after an experience with you becomes your trademark."
—Jay Danzie

THERE IS ONE INDISPENSABLE ingredient to great technical presentations. It is so important to your presentations that if you forget to include it, your presentation will be uncomfortable to deliver, sound flat to the audience, and will make you decrease your credibility.

You have been practicing it your entire life and probably don't give it a second thought.

Think of past times in your life when you were successful. What was the one ingredient crucial to your success?

That ingredient was YOU!

You are faced with delivering that big presentation. Your work colleague, Bob, says, "Everything will work out if you just be yourself." Well, something happens to us when we are in the workplace. Our personalities change to fit in, we start reacting to situations differently than we would otherwise, and we act as the boss would like us to act and not as we would act normally. In other words, we are not ourselves. You may do the same in your presentations.

If you do not inject yourself into your presentation preparation and delivery, you are in real danger of your presentation not having the effect you intended.

There has never been and never will be anyone exactly like you with your triumphs, your failures, and your life experiences. Don't leave these "at the door" when you prepare and deliver your presentations.

Your (1) enthusiasm for your subject area, (2) your experiences working in your subject area, and (3) your perspective on how you see your subject area today and, in the future, will make your presentation authentic, powerful, and interesting for the audience.

ENTHUSIASM

You have undoubtedly been in the audience when the speaker is not enthusiastic about his or her subject. Were you able to get enthusiastic about the subject? My educated guess is no.

Being enthusiastic for your subject doesn't guarantee everyone in the audience will be as enthusiastic, but not being enthusiastic about your subject almost always guarantees the audience will not be.

Talk in your regular conversational tone when you speak. Let your enthusiasm come out through your words, tone of voice, and especially your body language, and you will experience a great reaction from your audience.

EXPERIENCE

Audiences will love to hear your real-world experiences relevant to your presentation. Explain how you have experienced the subject from your years of experience using stories.

If you have been in your subject area for decades, you may want to relate what the subject area was like when you started your career, when you were at mid-career, and then, finally, where you see the subject area now.

PERSPECTIVE

Your experience in your subject area gives you a unique perspective on its future. It is a unique perspective because no one has had the exact same experiences you have. Share these experiences with your audiences but ensure these experiences support one or more of your main points.

Perhaps your experiences include the hopes of the subject area community when you were starting your career being realized later in your career. Were these hopes realized? Tell your audience why not.

There is a danger when you speak of something you are enthusiastic about, in which you have real life experience, and in which you predict the future. The presentation may get away from you. There is a saying in public speaking circles, "Don't fall in love with the sound of your voice." Say what you have to say and sit down.

The one indispensable ingredient in great presentation preparation and delivery is YOU. Inject all of your enthusiasm, your experience, and your perspective on the future of your subject area into your presentations.

You will have the time of your life, and so will your audience!

CALL TO ACTION

- Be enthusiastic about your topic.
- Tell your audience personal stories related to your topic.
- Relay your unique perspective on the topic.

"Get action. Do things; be sane; don't fritter away your time; create, act, take a place wherever you are and be someone; get action."

—Theodore Roosevelt

ADVERSITY REVEALS GREAT SPEAKING TIPS!

"Every problem has in it the seeds of its own solution. If you don't have any problems, you don't get any seeds."
—Norman Vincent Peale

"HOUSTON, WE HAVE A problem." Those were the words of astronaut Jack Swigert aboard the Apollo 13 spacecraft on April 13, 1970.

Apollo 13 was the seventh crewed mission in the Apollo space program and the third intended to land on the Moon. The craft was launched on April 11, 1970, from the Kennedy Space Center, Florida, but the lunar landing was aborted after an oxygen tank exploded two days later, crippling the service module (SM) upon which the command module (CM) had depended.

Despite great hardship caused by limited power, loss of cabin heat, shortage of potable water, and the critical need to make makeshift repairs to the carbon dioxide removal system, the crew returned safely to Earth on April 17, 1970, six days after launch. (Ref: Wikipedia, "Apollo 13")

So what does the Apollo 13 accident and recovery of the crew have to do with public speaking? Plenty. We can learn a number of things from the Apollo 13 astronauts that, if practiced diligently, will make us outstanding public speakers.

A PEACEFUL MIND GENERATES POWER

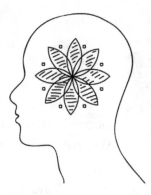

In the self-help classic *The Power of Positive Thinking* by Norman Vincent Peale, chapter two is entitled, "A Peaceful Mind Generates Power." Probably more often than not, when technical professionals have the prospect of preparing and delivering a presentation, there is a slow and, sometimes, not so slow buildup of stress during the presentation preparation period.

I am not a psychiatrist, but I have lived enough of life to know stress deteriorates your brain function. As an engineer, I fall back on my structured way of thinking when I am under stress. I look for solutions instead of problems. That is exactly what the Apollo 13 flight and ground crew did. Remember the classic line from Apollo 13 Flight Director Gene Krantz: "Failure is not an option."

How many times are we our own worst enemy when preparing for a presentation, telling ourselves bad self-talk such as "This will never work" or "I don't see where I have enough time to prepare for this presentation" or "I will look like a fool giving this presentation?" You fill in your words.

Remember, the audience does not know when you have left out a part of your presentation or forgot to credit a quote to a person or shortened your closing because you forgot half of it.

Read chapter two of *The Power of Positive Thinking* and your peaceful mind will generate the power you need to prepare and deliver an outstanding presentation.

NEVER GIVE IN

On October 29, 1941, after leading the survival of Great Britain in the Battle of Britain and still facing the Nazi menace, Winston Churchill, the Prime Minister of Great Britain, gave the commencement address at the Harrow School, his alma mater. In his closing remarks, he said this: "Never give in. Never give in. Never, never, never, never—in nothing, great or small, large or petty—never give in, except to convictions of honor and good sense. Never yield to force. Never yield to the apparently overwhelming might of the enemy."

But who is your enemy when preparing your presentation? Your enemy is your set of doubts about yourself you have accumulated over your lifetime! Your job is to slay these doubts and triumph like Churchill and Great Britain did. So how can you do this?

Well, first you have to realize that when you create a presentation, all the doubts about you that you have ever felt in your life will come to the forefront. It is kind of like the old commercial on TV where the person is trying to decide something with an angel on one shoulder and a devil on the other shoulder. The angel represents all the possibilities of ways to prepare and deliver an outstanding presentation, and the devil represents all the doubts you have ever accumulated in your life.

Most people are aware that action follows thought. We think about wanting a book, so we go to the bookstore and buy it. Not many people realize that thought can also follow action. Norman Vincent Peale once said, "If you want a quality, act as if you already have it. If you want to be courageous, act as if you were—and as you act and persevere in acting, so you tend to become." In other words, act "as if."

Act with yourself, with the people you meet, and in your presentation delivery as though you are an outstanding speaker. With repetition of these actions, your thoughts will gradually turn to solutions for your speaking challenges, and you will open your mind and see solutions that heretofore were hidden to you.

Never give in to your doubts and fears. Remember, courage is not feeling fear; courage is feeling fear and fighting through it.

HUMAN INGENUITY

So how did the ground and flight crew fix the problem aboard Apollo 13?

The big problem was the astronauts were inhaling oxygen and exhaling carbon dioxide. If the air in the command module was not constantly purified of the carbon dioxide, it would be deadly. The ground and flight crew improvised a way to join the Lithium-Hydroxide cube-shaped filter canisters to the lunar module's cylindrical canister-sockets by drawing air through them with a suit return hose. It was a brilliant and risky endeavor, but it worked.

Reward without risk does not exist. I am not sure if any of you have ever experienced the harrowing experience of the

Apollo 13 astronauts, but I bet you have felt jitters and, maybe, outright sickness before you give a presentation. Human ingenuity is not the only province of the Apollo 13 ground and aircrew. It is yours, too!

***

The traits of the astronauts using their peaceful minds, never giving in, and using their ingenuity can be readily applied to preparing and delivering an outstanding presentation.

Risk smartly and reap the rewards!

CALL TO ACTION

- Calm your mind to generate your greatest thinking power.
- Never give in to reach your present goals.
- Think "out of the box" to solve your current challenge.

"'Compared with what we ought to be, we are only half awake. Our fires are damped; our drafts are checked. We are making use of only a small part of our possible mental and physical resources.' Stating the thing broadly, he went on to write: 'The human individual thus lives usually far within his limits; he possesses powers of various sorts which he habitually fails to use. He energizes below his maximum, and he behaves below his optimum.'"

—William James in his essay
"On Vital Reserves"

YOUR PRESENTATION "PAIN POINTS!"

"The gap between what's expected and what you deliver is where the magic happens, in business and in life."

—Jay Baer

FOR THIS CHAPTER, I am going to shift emphasis a bit. I will tell you what were the three biggest "pain points" I had to overcome when I previously prepared and delivered presentations and how I solved them. I invite you to reply back to info@ speakleadandsucceed.com and tell me what your biggest "pain points" are with regard to your presentations.

Here are the three biggest "pain points" I had to overcome:

PAIN POINT #1: HOW CAN I DESIGN A PRESENTATION WITHIN A SPECIFIC MAXIMUM TIME?

This used to be a major stumbling block for me. I have been a Toastmaster for a while. In Toastmasters, you are taught that every presentation whether five minutes or an hour in length should contain three main points. This is a good rule of thumb. Less than three points will leave the audience wanting more information. More than three points will be hard for the audience to follow. These three main points are integral to the timing of your presentation.

These three main points plus supporting sub-points are the body of your speech and, coupled with your opening and closing, are your complete presentation.

My electronics shop teacher from high school use to say, "Divide and conquer." Any task, in this case preparing a presentation, can be divided (opening, body, closing) and developed separately to prepare the speech.

You can separately time the opening, body, and closing to stay within your maximum time of the presentation. Remember, though, the majority of the time of your presentation should be in the body of the presentation. The opening should introduce your topic and heighten the audience's anticipation of the speech. The closing should summarize the three main points and leave the audience with a call to action.

PAIN POINT #2: HOW DO YOU DECIDE WHAT TO INCLUDE IN MY PRESENTATION?

This is a perennial challenge for beginning and experienced speakers. Begin by choosing your proposed topic. I say "proposed" topic, because during your presentation preparation you may find the topic morphing a bit.

Next, write all the things you can think of pertaining to your topic without considering what your three main points will be. Brian Tracy, the self-development expert, calls this mind storming, which is similar to brainstorming but you do it by yourself.

Next, arrange all the ideas into three groups. These three groups will become your three main points. You may want to use the previously mentioned Cards on the Wall exercise. Remember, in the Cards on the Wall exercise, you put all the things pertaining to your topic on different Post-it notes ("yellow stickies"). Then you will simply put similar ideas in the same group. Voila! You have your three main points with supporting points.

This brings us to Pain Point #3.

PAIN POINT #3: HOW CAN I GET RID OF VERBAL FILLERS SUCH AS "AHS" AND "UMS?"

 When I was in the Air Force, I remember a presentation where the speaker said multiple "ahs" and "ums." I stopped counting at ninety-eight "ahs" and "ums." Verbal fillers—including "ahs," "ums," repeated words, etc.—are caused by our mouth being ahead of our brains thinking what to say next. We say these verbal fillers without knowing we are saying them. An essential skill of any speaker is to stop talking and let the brain catch up with the next logical point to make.

During your presentation preparation phase, a fun, some would say frightening, way to cure this is to have someone use those New Year's Eve clickers whenever you say a verbal filler. Almost instantaneously, you will find yourself pausing, thinking, and then saying your next logical point.

***

The "pain points" I had to solve were (1) designing a presentation to a maximum time, (2) deciding what to include in my presentation, and (3) using verbal fillers such as "ah" and "um."

There are solutions for all your pain points. Let me help you solve them.

Please reply back to info@speakleadandsucceed.com and tell me what your biggest "pain points" are with regard to your presentations.

CALL TO ACTION

- To ensure meeting the maximum time for a presentation, separately time your opening, each of your three main points, and your closing.
- Use mind storming to generate ideas to include in your presentation and then categorize these ideas into subpoints to your three main points.
- Give a New Year's Eve party clicker to a trusted friend in the audience who will click the clicker every time you utter a verbal filler.

"Ninety percent of how well the talk will go is determined before the speaker steps on the platform."

—Somers White

PART III: PRESENTATION PREPARATION (SPECIFIC)

PART II OF THIS book covered the prerequisites to prepare to win in your presentation. You could say this part is at the "twenty-five thousand–foot level" of presentation preparation. Part III of this book gets down to the "one thousand–foot level" of presentation. It talks about specific items you can do to aid your presentation preparation.

Here is where you discover whether you have "the will to prepare to win," according to Bear Bryant. Here is where "the rubber meets the ramp." Here you will practice the very things you will do in your actual presentation. We will get down into the "nitty gritty" of presentation preparation.

Part III covers the following topics:

- Speak Powerfully with Power Words!
- Audience-Catching Presentation Openings!
- Common Speech Errors Can Derail Your Presentation!

- Speaking Secrets of a Great Speaker!
- "Tell Me a Story, Daddy!"
- Speech Pattern Magic!
- Twenty Proven Ways to Reduce Your Fear of Public Speaking
- Increase Your Influence With the "Rule of Three!"
- Bridge Your Generational Divide!
- Why Only Some Speakers Succeed

SPEAK POWERFULLY WITH POWER WORDS!

*"Courage is what it takes to stand up and speak;
courage is also what it takes to sit down and listen."*
—Winston Churchill

IN THIS CHAPTER, WE will explore "The 5 Most Effective Words and Phrases in Public Speaking" (https://www.linkedin. com/pulse/5-most-effective-words-phrases-public-speaking-lucas-asu/) from the website article of the same name.

You have all heard the phrase, "The pen is mightier than the sword." Men and women throughout history have changed the lives of millions of people by the words they used. So what are the five most effective words and phrases in public speaking? Read on.

THE WORD "IMAGINE"

 This is the most powerful and influential word in the English language. Each person has a unique definition of "success" that he/she imagines and hopes someday to achieve. It personalizes the desires and dreams of each person that hears it. The word "imagine" derives its power from the fact that it's an open, non-restrictive command that invites the audience to imagine whatever they want.

And as they imagine in the context you have suggested, their own imagination (sense experience) starts doing the most important work—convincing themselves and, therefore, justifying why they should buy what you are offering or agreeing with your point of view.

John F. Kennedy once asked us to imagine landing a man on the moon, and a decade later, that imagining became a reality. By asking us to imagine, he was asking us to think of the possibilities and to convince ourselves that it's a possible and worthy endeavor to pursue. And we did. This is persuasion at its finest.

THE WORD "BREAKTHROUGH"

The word "breakthrough" expresses and describes the most radical, significant innovation people have been waiting for and dreaming of. It suggests a complete game-changing event—something they have never seen or experienced before that is offering meaning to their lives on several levels.

The late Steve Jobs, one of the most innovative leaders of our time, took full advantage of this powerful word during the launch of the iPhone in 2007. "We are just at the beginning stages of what will be truly remarkable breakthrough," he said. "The iPhone is a breakthrough in mobile technology."

THE PHRASE "YOU HAVE THE RIGHT TO"

The concept of "rights" is enshrined in the minds of all people that live in a democratic and open society. When you deploy the phrase "you have the right to," you immediately grab people's complete attention and raise their expectations of what they demand of themselves.

It is like you are giving them the license to demand more from themselves, to desire to have more of what they want out of life, and to become more than what they are. The phrase is effective and influential because it is intrinsic in our nature to become more. People will listen with greater interest when what you said reaffirms their own core beliefs.

Using this phrase "you have the right to" adds intensity to your message. When you communicate and relate your product, service, or idea into a "right," you go beyond selling it for its reasonable and beneficial factors; you are telling people it's an essential part of who they are and what they deserve.

THE PHRASE "LIFE-CHANGING IMPACT"

When you use the phrase "life-changing impact," you are implying that there will be a permanent and personalized benefit to the individual. It is imperative that when you use this phrase, you immediately demonstrate the extraordinary value of your service, product, or idea and contextualize it as a personal benefit that will enhance a person's quality of life.

In a La Francophonie Conference on Education, Michaelle Jean, the Secretary General of La Francophonie and former Governor General of Canada, said, "Education can have a life-changing impact on students."

THE PHRASE "A FORENSIC APPROACH"

 This phrase has been popularized by the hit TV series *CSI*. It is used to demonstrate the seriousness and strategic importance of your proposed approach. The power of this phrase is that it indicates a more detailed, precise, and clinical process of doing things that guarantees reliable, dependable, and predictable outcomes.

***

The five power words and phrases are:

- Imagine
- Breakthrough
- You have the right to
- Life-changing impact
- A forensic approach

Use these power words and greatly connect with your audience!

CALL TO ACTION

- Use the word "imagine" to engender possibilities in your audience members' minds.
- Use the word "breakthrough" to engender anticipation in your audience members' minds.
- Use the phrase "life-changing impact" to imply a permanent and personal benefit to audience members.

"Practice, practice, PRACTICE in speaking before
an audience will tend to remove all fear of
audiences, just as practice in swimming will lead to
confidence and facility in the water. You must learn
to speak by speaking."

—Dale Carnegie

AUDIENCE-CATCHING PRESENTATION OPENINGS!

"A wise man speaks because he has something to say, a fool speaks because he has to say something."

—Plato

IN THE FIRST THIRTY seconds of meeting you, your audience has formed their first impression of you. This first impression will be the basis for determining whether your presentation was successful or not. The opening of your presentation forms this first impression.

This chapter will discuss the benefits of a great opening, how your opening sets the tone of how your audience will feel about your presentation, and, finally, the different forms of your presentation opening.

WHAT ARE THE BENEFITS OF A GREAT OPENING?

Dorothy Leeds in her seminal book on public speaking, *Power Speak*, tells us, "Powerful speakers start powerfully. You must gain the audience's attention and interest the moment you walk on stage. Without that attention, you won't get your message across, you'll have trouble sustaining whatever interest there is, and you won't have established your leadership and control—the keys to being a powerful speaker."

Wow! Are those powerful words? Gaining the audience's attention is key. Without it, you will be "playing catchup" throughout your presentation.

You want to grab the audience's attention because it will determine the connection you have with the audience. You want to have the total undivided attention of your audience. It starts with your presentation opening.

Another benefit of a great opening in your presentations is it puts you and your audience at ease. Why is it important that your audience is at ease? Audiences at ease are more attentive and more willing to accept your main points. You can better influence them with a great opening. At ease audiences smile more. This has the added benefit of motivating you as a speaker.

It may be obvious, but if you are at ease, you will be more enthusiastic, present a better presentation, and have more fun doing it. Having fun actually opens up yours and your audience's minds, which will again cause you to have a better presentation.

I think you can see why it is important for you to have a great presentation opening. Your presentation opening also sets the tone for how your audience will feel.

HOW YOUR OPENING SETS THE TONE OF HOW YOUR AUDIENCE WILL FEEL ABOUT YOUR PRESENTATION

 When you present in front of your audience, you are taking them on a journey, a journey in their mind using your main points as mileposts along the way.

Through your opening, you have the power to set the tone for how you want the audience to feel during and after your presentation. Do you want your audience to feel sad, mad, glad, or scared, etc.? You have the power in your opening to do this.

If you want them to feel sad, tell them a story of a child stricken with leukemia who fights a valiant battle, loses the fight at age ten, but teaches us all about the will to live and what is really important in life.

If you want them to feel mad, tell them the statistics of illegal drug use in this country. Tell them how it is spreading in our schools to lower and lower grades each year. Tell them about the local and national laws that actually restrict our ability to fight this scourge.

If you want them to feel glad, talk to them about all the blessings we have in life. Tell them about the beauty of children and how we can all learn from them. Tell them about how you won your fight with pancreatic cancer.

If you want them to be scared, tell them about the scourge of child sexual abuse. Tell them how predators can be anyone. Tell them how the man in a trench coat in a myth. But also tell them there are definite and active ways to reduce the incidence of child sexual abuse.

My point in giving you these examples is to show you how you can engender certain feelings in your audience. You have the power to do this. Use it.

We have seen why it is important for you to have a great presentation opening and how your opening sets the tone of how your audience will feel about your presentation.

Now we will review the basic forms of the presentation opening.

WHAT ARE THE BASIC FORMS OF THE PRESENTATION OPENING?

Although not an exhaustive list, the following opening forms are the basic forms of the presentation opening. They have been time tested to grab an audience's attention.

-  *Stories:* Everyone loves a good story. Before there were iPhones, Snapchat, television, newspapers, radio, there were stories. I am sure you have seen prehistoric etchings on the walls of caves. Those etchings tell a story and enthralled the audience at the time.

-  *Quotes:* Quotes are powerful because they make us take a mental break and think. My favorite quotes are those from world leaders throughout the ages—George Washington, Abraham Lincoln, Winston Churchill, to name a few. Don't know any famous relevant quotes? Google the word "quotes," and you will get more quotes than you can possibly use.

-  **_Statistics:_** Statistics can immediately change how people think about things. For instance, most people think suicide rates actually skyrocket around Christmastime. In reality, the Center for Disease Control (CDC) actually reports that suicide rates are actually lowest in December. The suicide rate actually peaks in the spring, not the winter. Statistics are powerful. Make sure they are relevant to your presentation.

-  **_Humor:_** Earl Nightingale said, "The only requirement for a speaker is to be interesting." Laughing actually opens your and your audience's minds because when we laugh, we are open to more ideas from others. The author Norman Cousins actually helped cure himself of a terrible sickness by watching videotapes of comedian teams like the Three Stooges, Laurel and Hardy, and Abbott and Costello.

-  **_Rhetorical Questions:_** Rhetorical questions, of course, are questions not meant to be answered by your audience. They are questions that provoke thought, such as, "Have you ever thought about how your heritage affects your point of view?" or "What should be humanity's goal?" or "If you could teach the entire world just one concept, what would it be?" These questions open the minds of your audience and provide you with multiple paths in which to take your presentation.

-  ***A Personal Experience:*** Audiences love to hear about your personal experiences. It makes you human and approachable. A personal foible of yours will be particularly loved by your audience. Experiment and don't be afraid to poke fun at yourself. The rewards from this are plenty.

We have learned the benefits of a great opening, how your opening sets the tone of how your audience feels about your presentation, and the basic forms of the presentation opening.

Remember, you only get one chance to make a first impression. Use your presentation opening to make the best first impression possible!

CALL TO ACTION

- Grab your audience's attention in your opening and don't let it go for the rest of your presentation.
- Establish in your opening how you want your audience to feel throughout your presentation.
- Use the basic forms in your presentation opening: stories, quotes, statistics, humor, rhetorical questions.

"You can tell if a man is clever by his answers. You can tell if a man is wise by his questions."

—Anonymous

COMMON SPEECH ERRORS CAN DERAIL YOUR PRESENTATION!

"The goal of effective communication should be for listeners to say 'Me too!' versus 'So what?'"

—Jim Rohn

LET'S FACE IT. THE real reason we engineers and scientists do not get English degrees is that we are more comfortable with numbers than we are with words. There is no doubt the efforts of engineers and scientists over a number of centuries have brought us to our present wonderful standard of living.

However, think about what would have happened if Madame Curie, who discovered radium, or if Alexander Graham Bell, who invented the telephone, or if Marconi, who pioneered the wireless radio, had not properly communicated the value of X-rays, the telephone, and wireless radio. Would we be at the state of technology we are now? Maybe, maybe not.

As proud I am to be an engineer, our ability to speak and write correctly will have a profound effect on our success in all areas of our lives. Earl Nightingale in his program Lead the Field said, "A person may dress in the latest fashion and present a very attractive appearance. But the minute he or she opens his or her mouth and begins to speak, he or she proclaims to the world his or her level on the socio-economic pyramid." It's true.

The way we speak tells others where we fit in society and whether others should listen to what we say. In addition to being an engineer, I am a speaker and writer. I have to admit high school English was not my favorite subject. However, as I have matured over my adult life, I rely ever-increasingly on my ability to write and speak well. In fact, in my observation, writing and speaking well is the most portable job skill you can have. Every occupation requires varying amounts of writing and speaking in addition to influencing others.

A book I read a number of years ago was an informative and surprisingly interesting one on proper English usage. The book, entitled *You Don't Say!* by Dr. Tom Parks, highlights the top ten mistakes people make in speech and writing. Space precludes me telling you the full ten; however, I will briefly describe three of these mistakes of English usage and how to correct them as Dr. Parks has outlined them.

"YOU" AND "I," "YOU" AND "ME"

Suppose you are going to take a cab to the airport for a business trip. You are going on the business trip with a colleague. Let's call him Doug. You might say to your spouse, "Honey, a cab will take

Doug and I to the airport." If you were the only one taking the cab to the airport, you would probably say, "Honey, a cab will take me to the airport." Now in one sentence you used "I" and in another sentence you used "me." Which one is correct? The sentence using "me" is correct. The sentence using "I" is incorrect. Adding Doug to the sentence does not change the status of the pronoun "me." The correct way to say the first sentence would be, "Honey, a cab will take Doug and me to the airport."

"WHO" AND "WHOM"

 Who has not agonized over these two English language gems? These words have competed for inclusion in sentences for as far as I can remember. I have to tell you, I still got them confused before reading Dr. Parks' book. In a nutshell, "who" is the correct word to use if the word used is referring to the one who acts such as, "Who did they think would win the game?" In this sentence, the word "who" is referring to who was winning the game (the one who acts).

It is correct to use "whom" if this word refers to the one who is acted upon such as in, "Give the book to whom you choose." In this sentence, "whom" is receiving the book (the one who is acted upon).

Remember, "who" is used for the one who acts and "whom" is used for the one who is acted upon.

"EVERYBODY" IS NOT PLURAL

At face value, you would probably say the sentence, "Everybody brought their own umbrella," is correct. However, if you did, you would be violating the English grammar rule of subject-object number agreement. The word "everybody" means every single body, not all-single bodies. The problem with this sentence is the word "everybody" is singular while the word "their" is plural.

In the sentence, the subject, "everybody," and the object, "their," must both be either singular or both be plural since they refer to the same person(s). Therefore, the correct form of the sentence would be, "Everybody brought his or her own umbrella." Correct speaking separates the "haves" and the "have-nots" in this world.

***

The next time you speak, ensure you broadcast to the world you know proper English usage. Proper English is a necessary part of your public speaking and directly contributes to whether you influence your audience favorably or not.

CALL TO ACTION

- Use the proper use of "You" and "I," "You" and "Me."
- Use the proper use of "Who" and "Whom."
- Use the proper use of "Everybody."

"The royal road to a man's heart is to talk to him about the things he treasures most."

—Dale Carnegie

SPEAKING SECRETS OF A GREAT SPEAKER!

"He mobilized the English language and sent it into battle to steady his fellow countrymen and hearten those Europeans upon whom the long dark night of tyranny had descended."
—Edward R. Murrow, on Winston Churchill, 1954

WHAT DID EDWARD R. Murrow mean in the above quote when he said of Winston Churchill, "He mobilized the English language and sent it into battle. . . ?" Mr. Murrow meant by Winston Churchill's speeches during the dark days of the Nazi "blitz" and all during World War II that he galvanized the will of the English people to fight on even to the point of death to eradicate the English Isles of the Nazi menace.

You all have heard the saying, "The pen is mightier than the sword." I posit that the spoken word is more powerful than the pen.

Your job as a presenter is to "galvanize" your audience into making their opinion of your topic their opinion. I can think of no better person that epitomizes exerting influence on their audience than Winston Churchill.

Below, I will examine three of Winston Churchill's speeches and how he used rhetorical devices to greatly influence his audience.

USE POWERFUL AND DESCRIPTIVE STATEMENTS

On May 13, 1940, Winston Churchill addressed Parliament about the frightening threat posed by Nazi Germany (winstonchurchill.org/resources/speeches/1940-the-finest-hour/blood-toil-tears-and-sweat-2/). He had just been appointed Prime Minister of England. He was attempting to prepare England for the road ahead in the face of Nazi aggression.

My point here is not to give you a history lesson, but to examine different parts of Winston Churchill's speech to Parliament and point out rhetorical devices he used in this speech that you can use in your speeches.

In the late William Safire's book *Lend Me Your Ears*, he points out the following description by Winston Churchill of the Nazi menace: "a monstrous tyranny never surpassed in the dark and lamentable catalogue of human crime." Wow! What a powerfully descriptive statement. Can you make the statements in your presentation more descriptive and powerful?

Mr. Churchill shows what he and his new government have to offer by saying, "I say to the House as I said to ministers who have joined this government, I have nothing to offer by blood, toil, tears, and sweat. We have before us an ordeal of the most grievous kind. We have before us many, many months of struggle and suffering."

So what does Mr. Churchill do in this section of his speech? Notice he uses alliteration: "many, many months of struggle and suffering." Why does he do this? Because alliteration is easier to remember for the audience. Remember, Churchill wanted this speech to resonate in the minds of Members of Parliament far after his speech was done.

If Churchill had had one good speech with his future speeches lackluster, he could have been dismissed as a "one hit wonder." But that was not Churchill's way. He realized the English language could be "mobilized" to move the hearts and minds of his country's citizens to steel them for the difficult months and years ahead.

On May 26, 1940, the evacuation of Dunkirk started with the Royal Air Force playing a major role in denying the Nazis air supremacy in the skies over Dunkirk. It was hoped forty-five thousand Allied troops could be evacuated. At the end of the Dunkirk evacuation, three hundred thirty-eight thousand Allied troops were evacuated.

USE REPEATED WORDS TO "HIT HOME" YOUR POINTS WITH YOUR AUDIENCE

On June 4, 1940, Winston Churchill reported to the House of Commons on the Dunkirk evacuation (winstonchurchill. org/resources/speeches/1940-the-finest-hour/we-shall-fight-on-the-beaches/). He talked about the struggle. He said,

"We shall go on to the end, we shall fight in France, we shall fight on the seas and oceans, we shall fight with growing confidence and growing strength in the air, we shall defend our Island, whatever the cost may be, we shall fight on the beaches, we shall fight on the landing grounds, we shall fight in the fields and in the streets, we shall fight in the hills; we shall never surrender. . . "

What can you learn from this quote? Notice how Churchill keeps repeating, "We shall fight. . . " If you have to make sure something "hits home" in your speech, repeat the words you want to "hit home" repeatedly.

Churchill goes on in the speech, saying,

". . . and even if, which I do not for a moment believe, this Island or a large part of it were subjugated and starving, then our Empire beyond the seas, armed and guarded by the British Fleet, would carry on the struggle, until, in God's good time, the New World, with all its power and might, steps forth to the rescue and the liberation of the old."

This is an example showing his sincerity in believing that in the end, the British Empire would have the resources to beat down the Nazis. You have to believe in what you are saying in your presentations before the audience will believe it.

This example of Churchill's speaking also points out that you are most convincing when you are yourself. Churchill made a career of being himself. You can also.

From July to October 1940, the Battle of Britain, the fight for air supremacy over the skies of Britain, was waged.

USE THE "RULE OF THREE" TO MAKE YOUR POINTS MORE EASILY REMEMBERED

On August 20, 1940, Churchill again addressed the House of Commons. (winstonchurchill.org/resources/speeches/1940-the-finest-hour/the-few/)

During the speech, he praised the airmen of the RAF by saying this:

> *"The gratitude of every home in our Island, in our Empire, and indeed throughout the world, except in the abodes of the guilty, goes out to the British airmen who, undaunted by odds, unwearied in their constant challenge and mortal danger, are turning the tide of the World War by their prowess and by their devotion."*

Wow! In the field of public speaking, Churchill is a superstar. Notice his use of the words "except in the abodes of the guilty," meaning the Nazis. Very powerful.

In the same speech, he went on to say, "Never in the field of human conflict was so much owed by so many to so few."

Notice how he uses the terms "so much," "so many," and just when you are expecting a superlative, Churchill comes back with the limited words, "to so few." Try this in your speaking. Notice also, that he uses the rule of three. When you are speaking a list of terms, two terms seem not enough, four terms seem too much, but three terms seem just right. I invoked the rule of three in the last sentence.

***

What have you learned in this chapter about how we can emulate Winston Churchill as presenters?

- Use alliteration so it is easier for the audience to remember what you say.
- Use colorful words in your descriptions.
- "Mobilize" your language to win the hearts and minds of your audience.
- Repeatedly say the words you want to "hit home."
- Be sincere in what you believe—your audience will only believe what you are saying if you believe what you are saying.
- You are the most convincing when you are yourself.
- Use the rule of three to make your points more easily remembered by your audience.

You too can learn to move audiences like Winston Churchill did. Will it take practice? Of course, but practicing these methods will increasingly move your audiences. Isn't that why you are speaking?

CALL TO ACTION

- Use powerful and descriptive statements in your presentations.

- Use repeated words to "hit home" your main points with your audience.
- Use the Rule of Three to make your points more easily remembered.

"Of all the talents bestowed upon men, none is so precious as the gift of oratory. He who enjoys it wields a power more durable than that of a great king. He is an independent force in the world."

—Winston Churchill

"TELL ME A STORY, DADDY!"

"A compelling story beats a mountain of facts every time. Stories don't have to be amazing, incredible tales—often family mishaps and personal insights are very moving."
—Dorothy Leeds from her book, Power Speak

ARE YOU A STORYTELLER?

If you told your wife about your day at work, you are a storyteller.

If you reminisced to your husband about the first bike you received as a child, you are a storyteller.

If you told your co-worker about the guy who cut you off on your way to work, you are a storyteller.

We are all storytellers. Why is storytelling vital to connecting with your audience? We will explore how stories grab the attention of your audience, give your audience "hooks" to remember the main points of your presentation, and finally, how your stories tap into the emotions of your audience to make your presentations memorable.

STORIES GRAB THE ATTENTION OF YOUR AUDIENCE

What is the purpose of your presentation opening? The purpose is to "grab" your audience's attention. One of the best ways to grab their attention is to tell a story in your opening.

Why were the movies *Gone with the Wind*, *The Godfather*, and *Star Wars* such blockbuster successes? They grabbed your attention because the stories they led you through were compelling, enthralling, and riveting. You really did not know what was coming next.

You want the same emotions for your audiences. You want to keep them on the edge of their seats in anticipation of what is to come in your presentation.

The late Paul Harvey was a master storyteller. He was able to mask the name of the subject of his stories with such legerdemain that after he told you at the end of his story who the story's subject was, you probably said to yourself, "Of course, that is who it was." Paul Harvey used the power of story to lure you in and increase your anticipation as the story unfolded. It was a true gift. Google on the following phrase for an example of Paul Harvey's story mastery: "The Constitution—those who signed it and at what cost." Use Paul Harvey's technique to get your audience to focus on your presentation.

Stories grab your audience's attention. They also give your audience "hooks" so they can remember your main points.

STORIES GIVE YOUR AUDIENCE "HOOKS" SO THEY CAN REMEMBER YOUR MAIN POINTS

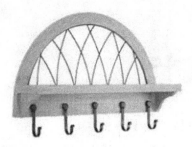

If you have ever read any books or articles on memory recall, you know recall is greatly aided by associating a certain thing to your memory. Stories can act as the thing that associates to your main points, thus allowing your audience to remember your main points more clearly.

Has anyone ever said to you, "Boy, wait until I tell you this story?" Sure you have. We are surrounded by stories every day. Whether the stories come from the news media, your colleague in the next cubicle or your wife or husband, they are all stories. Years later, you will remember these stories. My point here is your stories help your audience to remember your main points during and long after your presentation.

Make sure your stories are relevant to the part of your presentation you are giving when you tell the story and evoke the emotions you want the audience to feel. Your audience will remember your main points more if you tell stories supporting the main points.

The "hooks" your stories provide to your audience can be greatly enhanced if they evoke the emotions in your audience you intend.

STORIES TAP THE EMOTIONS OF YOUR AUDIENCE

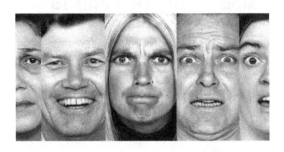

Remember when you were a small child. You couldn't read yet, but you sure loved the stories your mom or dad told you at bedtime. Why did you like them so much? Because slaying dragons or Thing 1/Thing 2 (refer to *The Cat in the Hat* by Dr. Seuss to find out what Thing 1/Thing 2 are) or finding out *Where the Wild Things Are* (by Maurice Sendak) tugged at your emotions and excited your imagination.

Let me ask you a question. Do you love a story told by a speaker if the story is relevant to the presentation and told with great emotion? Of course you do. School subjects such as math are dry because they are taught without appealing to students' emotions. Would math be more interesting if you told a story about the mathematician who invented or discovered the concept you are teaching? Of course it would.

Your audience doesn't necessarily remember what you say in your presentations, but they will remember how they feel. How they feel is all about their emotions during your presentation. You can tell your stories in such a way that they tap deeply into the emotions of audience members and thus make your presentation more memorable.

***

Why is storytelling vital to connecting with your audience? Your stories grab the attention of your audience, give your audience "hooks" to remember the main points of your presentation, and finally tap into the emotions of your audience to make your presentation more memorable.

So, are you a storyteller? You are.

Stories have great power in your presentations.

Use your stories to make your presentations the ones everyone is talking about!

CALL TO ACTION

- Use stories to grab your audience's attention.
- Use stories for your audience to use as "hooks" so they can remember your main points.
- Use stories to tap into your audience's emotions.

"We're all storytellers. We tell stories to sell our ideas. We tell stories to motivate teams. We tell stories to encourage our children to reach their full potential."

—Carmine Gallo from his book The Storyteller's Secrets: From TED Speakers to Business Legends, Why Some Ideas Catch on and Others Don't

SPEECH PATTERN MAGIC!

*"The success of your presentation will be judged not by
the knowledge you send but by what
the listener receives."*

—Lilly Walters

WE HAVE TALKED A lot about speaking. However, one public speaking topic we have not covered is the common speech patterns you can use to organize your presentations. Speech patterns are very helpful because they guide you when you are preparing and delivering your presentation and the audience in hearing your presentation.

What follows are the common speech patterns, how the speech pattern you have selected for your presentation actually increases your influence with your audience, and how you can adapt different speech patterns to the same presentation.

WHAT ARE THE COMMON SPEECH PATTERNS?

The following information on speech patterns comes from What Are the Five Organizational Patterns of Public Speaking (bizfluent.com/info-8540323-five-organizational-patterns-public-speaking.html).

- <u>Logical or Topical</u>. If you are giving a presentation that contains several ideas that are interrelated in such a way that one flows naturally to the next, the logical pattern of organization can be used. As the name implies, you'll be organizing the information in a logical manner according to topic. This organizational pattern can also be used in a speech that discusses several sub-topics under the banner of a primary topic—just attack them all in a logical sequence.

- <u>Chronological</u>. When information in a speech follows a chronological sequence, then the information should likewise be organized chronologically. For example, a speech on the development of a new technology should begin with its origin, then continue along the same timeline as events occurred. This organizational pattern is typically used in any speech addressing a subject from a historical perspective.

- <u>Geographical</u>. If you wish to evoke an image of something that has various parts and those parts are distinguished by geography, then organize your speech using a spatial pattern. Spatial patterns are suited for speeches about a country or city or even a building or organization, provided that the organization occupies a specific geographical location, such as a hospital or university.

- <u>Cause-and-Effect</u>. Another way of organizing a speech on a particular topic is to look at the subject in terms of cause and effect. For example, a speech about providing foreign aid to victims of a natural disaster in another country would discuss the disaster itself (the cause) and the impact the disaster had on the nation's people (the effect). In this particular example, a further effect would be found in discussing the details of how foreign aid can help the victims.
- <u>Problem-Solution</u>. The problem-solution organizational pattern is similar to the cause-and-effect pattern but is typically used when the speaker is trying to persuade the audience to take a particular viewpoint. In essence, the speaker introduces a problem and then outlines how this problem can be solved.

There you have the five basic speech patterns you can use in your presentations. Read on to find out how you can use speech patterns to increase your influence with your audience.

HOW USING SPEECH PATTERNS INCREASE YOUR INFLUENCE WITH YOUR AUDIENCE

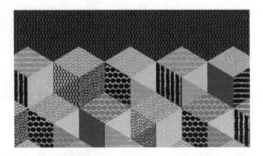

Once you have selected the appropriate speech pattern, it will greatly help you in preparing your presentations because they suggest the main points of your presentation and their order. The basic speech patterns are akin to a roadmap of your presentation.

Just as speech patterns guide you through your presentation preparation, speech patterns will also guide your audience through your presentation. It will not take long for your audience to realize there is a pattern to your presentation.

A recognizable pattern allows your audience to focus on your message. Haphazard presentation patterns distract your audience, focusing them on the haphazard nature of your presentation and defocusing them on your message.

Audiences love to listen to presentations that follow familiar speech patterns. Because of the familiar organization of your presentation, you actually will increase your credibility with your audience. Increasing your credibility will increase your influence with your audience.

We have explored the basic speech patterns and how you can use speech patterns to increase your influence with your audience. Let's now look at how you can adapt different speech patterns to the same presentation.

HOW YOU CAN ADAPT DIFFERENT SPEECH PATTERNS TO THE SAME PRESENTATION

You may be thinking that the speech pattern you choose for your presentation cannot be changed to another speech pattern.

Although the five speech patterns are different and unique, with a little imagination and effort you can change one speech pattern to another in the same presentation.

For instance, your presentation about the great museums of Italy can follow a chronological pattern (e.g., Tuesday: visiting the Vatican Museums in Rome; Wednesday: visiting the Gallery of the Academy of Florence (Galleria dell'Accademia di Firenze) where the David is; Thursday: visiting the Doge's Palace in Venice, and so on).

You could easily turn this chronological speech pattern in your presentation about the great museums of Italy into the geographical speech pattern by emphasizing the cities in which the great museums reside: Rome, Florence, and Venice.

You could also easily turn this chronological speech pattern in your presentation about the great museums of Italy into the logical/topical speech pattern by emphasizing the museums themselves.

The same topic can be portrayed in your presentation using many different speech patterns.

There is a caution, though. Use only one speech pattern in your presentation. If you try to mix two or more speech patterns in your presentation, you will only end up confusing your audience and yourself when you deliver your presentation. Remember, the speech pattern is a map of your presentation for the audience.

***

We have defined the five basic speech patterns: (1) logical or topical, (2) chronological or time-sequenced, (3) spatial or geographical, (4) cause-and-effect, and (5) problem-solution; showed how speech patterns actually add to your influence with your audience; and finally, explained how to adapt speech patterns to the same presentation.

If you stick to one of these basic speech patterns, presentation preparation will be easier, and you will give your audience the gift of listening to a well-organized presentation, which will always be appreciated by audiences.

CALL TO ACTION

- Use the following common speech patterns to structure your presentations: logical or topical, chronological, geographical, cause-and-effect, problem-solution.
- Give your audiences a roadmap to follow your presentations by using one of the common speech patterns.
- Experiment by adapting your presentation to more than one common speech pattern.

"Let thy speech be better than silence, or be silent."

—Dionysius of Halicarnassus

TWENTY PROVEN WAYS TO REDUCE YOUR FEAR OF PUBLIC SPEAKING

"Do the thing you fear most and the death of fear is certain."

—Mark Twain

WHEN PEOPLE ARE SURVEYED for their greatest fears, the fear of speaking in public consistently is listed as the number one fear, even more than the fear of death. Believe it or not!

We all feel the fear of speaking in public to some extent. The question is how do you deal with this fear?

Below are twenty ways on how to deal with your fear of speaking in public:

1. Do the thing you fear repeatedly.
2. Everyone is somewhat fearful when they speak before an audience.
3. Most of the time, the thing you fear will not happen.
4. Fight your fear or else it will become a self-fulfilling prophecy.
5. Practice your speech ten to twenty times by yourself and then practice it another ten to twenty times by yourself— what you do in practice, you will do in public.
6. Practice your presentation before an audience of trusted friends.
7. Visit where you will give your presentation before you speak.
8. Realize your audience wants you to succeed.
9. If you are not a little bit fearful, your presentation will be flat.
10. Visualize a standing ovation from your audience.
11. The audience does not know, unless you tell them, when your presentation veers from how you practiced—don't tell them.
12. Realize you are the most knowledgeable about your topic.
13. Delivering a presentation is just one-on-one conversations one at a time with several people (your audience).
14. Imagine you are the boss of everyone in your audience.
15. Imagine you are a teacher and your audience is a kindergarten class.
16. Before your presentation, ask and answer every possible question that could be asked on your topic.
17. Realize your fear will energize you during your presentation.

18. According to Earl Nightingale, 92 percent of worries are things that happened in your past you have no control over or things that will never happen—stop worrying.
19. Talk to others about their fear of public speaking and what they did to overcome it.
20. Help another person overcome his or her fear of speaking in public.

***

Realize that the fear of speaking in public is a natural fear shared by millions and, maybe, billions of people around the world.

You have all heard the mantra, "You can't control what happens in your life, but you can always control your reaction to circumstances in your life." It is true. You always have a choice on how to react. Face your fear of public speaking and the death of this fear is certain!

CALL TO ACTION

- Practice your presentations over and over again and reduce your fear.
- Visit where you will deliver your presentation before you do.
- Don't waste time worrying. Ninety-two percent of your worries are from your past, which you can do nothing about or will never happen.

"A book may give you excellent suggestions on how best to conduct yourself in the water, but sooner or later you must get wet. . . "

—*Dale Carnegie*

INCREASE YOUR INFLUENCE WITH THE "RULE OF THREE!"

*"Courage is what it takes to stand up and speak.
Courage is also what it takes to sit down and listen."*
—*Winston Churchill*

 **YOU MAY NOT REALIZE** it, but most of the things that happen in your life happen in threes: you're born, you live, you die; you go to class, you take a test, you get a grade; you apply for a job, you get the job, you leave the job. It is called the Rule of Three.

When you read or hear someone speak, if the words on the page or the speaker's words are divided into three main parts, they are more easily remembered.

If you buy a new appliance, the instructions are usually divided into three parts: cautions, how to operate the appliance, and how to maintain the appliance.

If you are telling a story, there is a beginning, a middle, and an end.

You can solve a problem in three stages: define the problem, propose various solutions, select and implement one of the solutions.

Like other parts of life, there is magic in talking to people using the Rule of Three by having no more than three main points.

- **Your audience cannot remember more than three main points.** Are you more likely to remember the last three things or the last ten things you did today? The last three things you did today are much easier to remember than the last ten things you did today. Something happens to your audience if you ask them to remember four or more main points from your presentation. Asking your audience to remember four or more main points in your presentation starts to get confusing for your audience. They start confusing your main points. The confusion gets more intense as your number of main points rises. Don't do this to your audience and yourself!

- **Your audience will "tune out" after your third point**. There is a priest at my church whose homily drones on well past when the homily should have ended. The average homily in my church lasts ten minutes. However, this priest's homilies last at least twice as long. One day he spoke for twenty-five minutes. It was pure agony. So, what is wrong with speaking for twenty-five minutes with multiple main points more than three? You run the risk of your audience "tuning you out." We had a saying in the Air Force that is apropos: "Be bold, be brief, be gone!" Say what you need to say using three main points and then sit down!

- **Stories with three main points are memorable.** Do you remember the stories your parents used to read to you? Do you know why they were and are so memorable?

It is because in each of those stories, the authors used the Rule of Threes. The "Boy Who Cried Wolf" can be summed up in three parts: the boy cried wolf multiple times with the lumberjacks coming to his rescue, the last time the boy cried wolf it was for real, the lumberjacks did not come to his rescue. "Sleeping Beauty" can be summed up in three parts: Sleeping Beauty ate the poisoned apple given to her by the witch, Sleeping Beauty fell asleep, the prince awakened her with a kiss. Finally, "Goldilocks and the Three Bears" has multiple examples of the Rule of Three: three bears, three porridges, three beds. Apply this to your stories and your audiences will be mesmerized!

Having three main points in your presentation makes it easily remembered by your audience, will prevent or at least reduce the urge of your audience to "tune you out," and will make your stories memorable.

CALL TO ACTION

- Use no more than three main points to make your presentation more easily remembered by your audience.
- Use no more than three main points to reduce the chances of your audience "tuning you out."
- Use no more than three main points in your stories to make them memorable.

"Think twice before you speak, because your words and influence will plant the seed of either success or failure in the mind of the other."

—Napoleon Hill

BRIDGE YOUR GENERATIONAL DIVIDE!

"Only the prepared speaker deserves to be confident."
—Dale Carnegie

HAVE YOU EVER TALKED to a group somewhat homogeneous in generation and get a rousing standing ovation at the end of your presentation? And then you give the same talk to a somewhat homogeneous for an audience of a different generation from the first talk and your presentation fall flat? Have you ever wondered why this is so?

Well, different generations view life differently. Your presentation that works well for one generation may not work well for a different generation. Now, even within a generation, there are different views; however, as a speaker, it is important you understand the generation to which you are speaking.

Below are the characteristics of the five generations (from "GENERATIONAL BREAKDOWN: Info About All of the Generations – The Center for Generational Kinetics) and how to approach them in your presentation (from *Unlocking Generational Codes: Understanding What Makes the Generations Tick and What Ticks Them Off* by Anna Liotta).

Leadership Approaches for Generation Z come from "Generation Z Is Here: 3 Simple Tips Leaders Need to Know to Keep Them From Leaving" (INC. Magazine) by Marcel Schwantes.

TRADITIONALISTS OR SILENT GENERATION (BORN 1945 AND BEFORE)

Practical, dedicated, and loyal are adjectives that may describe the Silents who tend also to respect authority and work hard.

Preferred Approach: Directive, Logical, Authoritative
Plan: Clear, Precise
Long-Term Goal Style: Authoritative, Due Respect, Distant

BABY BOOMERS (BORN 1946-1964)

Competitive, focused and goal-oriented can characterize the Boomer generation. Some describe them as optimistic and disciplined and strong team players.

Preferred Approach: Consensual, Democratic, Process-Driven
Plan: Work with the "designated" group to define vision/mission
Style: Friendly "equals" open to input from appropriate leadership peers

GENERATION X (BORN 1965-1976)

Generation X tends to thrive on a balanced life. They have been described as self-reliant and pragmatic.

Preferred Approach: Competence, Results-Oriented
Plan: Project, Deadline, & Give People the Freedom to get it done
Style: Informal, Genuine, Bottom-Line

MILLENNIALS (BORN 1977-1995)

Hopeful, fun-seeking, and ambitious are among the characteristics that have been used to define this generation.

Preferred Approach: Collaborative, Experiential, Digital
Plan: Educational, Technically Savvy, "Gamer" Dive-In
Style: Achievement-Oriented, Positive, Fast

GENERATION Z (BORN 1996-TBD)

Entrepreneurial and tech savvy are two common characteristics of Generation Z. They tend to want independence and may be motivated by security. Multi-tasking could come naturally for this group.

Preferred Approach 1. Establish regular check-ins. Data shows that Gen Zers crave face time with their managers to reconnect and reset. Nine out of ten Gen Zers want frequent, face-to-face meetings with their managers. Weekly check-ins are Gen Zers' preferred cadence, according to Nintex data.

Preferred Approach 2. Make a point to discuss emotional well-being. One thousand full-time U.S. workers and five hundred U.S. managers were surveyed. According to their data, 90 percent of employees admit to performing better when their companies support their emotional wellness. But only 40 percent of managers make a point to ask about emotional wellness in one-on-ones. While past generations may have steered clear of emotional well-being topics at the office, Gen Zers approach the topic without fear. Additionally, 73 percent of Gen Zers take advantage of their organizations' employee assistance programs; only 24 percent of baby boomers do the same.

Preferred Approach 3. Invest in robust tech tools with a strong user experience (UX). Gen Zers will keep IT departments on their toes. As digital natives, they have high expectations for the technology they use at work. Not all work tools have a simple and stellar UX, and Gen Zers may get frustrated and find ways to work around certain tools. In fact, four out of five Gen Zers said they're willing to go against their companies' app policies if they believe their preference will work better.

***

The number one task for you as a speaker is to know your audience. Knowing what generations are in your audience and what they like, dislike, what they respond to most favorably, and what "turns them off" is critical to preparing and delivering your presentation effectively.

As the subtitle to Anna Liotta's book says, "Know what makes the generations in your audience tick, and most importantly, what ticks them off!"

CALL TO ACTION

- Determine well before your presentation what generations will be represented in your audience and in what rough number of each generation.
- Prepare and practice the delivery of your presentation that appeals to the generation(s) in your audience.
- Don't project during your presentation the characteristics of your generation unless that is the only generation in your audience.

*"Do not say a little in many words but a
great deal in a few."*

—Pythagoras

WHY ONLY SOME SPEAKERS SUCCEED

"Many attempts to communicate are nullified by saying too much."

—Robert Greenleaf

IN THE BOOK *OUTLIERS* by Malcolm Gladwell, the word "outlier" means (1) something that is situated away from or classed differently from a main or related body and (2) a statistical observation that is markedly different in value from the others of the sample.

Outliers is a fascinating book examining why certain people succeed while others don't. Gladwell's findings will surprise you! Success is not achieved by what you may be thinking.

As I read *Outliers*, I started thinking of the outlier speakers. These are the speakers than never want for work even in trying times. They mesmerize us from the stage and from their videos and books. We will pay a premium to hear them speak. They have star power. What separates them from the "pack?" Read on to find out.

10,000 HOURS

In *Outliers*, Gladwell explains there are people who are naturals at whatever activity they are pursuing. However, if they don't practice at a sufficient enough pace per week, they will never reach their full potential and will eventually be passed by those who, although not having natural ability, practice at a much higher tempo.

In fact, Gladwell studied this phenomenon and cites studies in *Outliers* that support the fact it takes about ten thousand hours' practice in whatever the activity is to become one of the truly best in the world at the activity. These are the celebrated concert pianist, the basketball star, or the world-renowned brain surgeon. Gladwell's research and those of others seems to support the ten thousand hours hypothesis.

Applying this to speakers, how many hours have you practiced your speaking? Practice, in this sense, means hours practicing before your presentations and the hours you actually have been delivering presentations. If you added all these hours, how close would you be to ten thousand hours?

So, following Gladwell's research, ten thousand hours seem to be required to become a world-class speaker, but it is not sufficient. Ten thousand hours presenting material to your audience they don't want and don't need will not put you in the top class of speakers.

KNOWING WHAT THE AUDIENCE WANTS AND NEEDS

Would you buy a car from a salesman that doesn't first determine your requirements for the car? Of course not! Then why would you want to listen to a speaker that doesn't understand your wants and needs? You wouldn't.

Then why would you as a speaker attempt to talk to an audience before understanding what they want and what they need? If you do, you will never rise to the heights of the great speakers. Great speakers "have their finger on the pulse" of their audience. They know what their audience wants, they know what they need, and they know how to deliver both.

If you know what your audience wants and needs, you will have a successful presentation. If you don't, you won't, and more importantly, you will not be asked back. It takes approximately seven times the effort to win the business of a new customer as it takes to win more business from an existing customer. Which is less effort? Your existing customers are your core. Treat them as the royalty they are!

Practicing ten thousand hours and giving your audience what they want and need will get you to passible speaker status. If you want to be a sought-after thought leader in your field, you must amaze and delight your audience. One great way to do this is to over deliver more than what your audience expects.

OVERDELIVER

A sure way to delight your audience and be asked back by the event planner is to overdeliver on your content. By overdeliver, I mean give your audience tangible tools and actions they can take to improve their personal and professional lives the minute they walk out of the room.

The key to success in speaking is to give your audience much more in use value than the price of admission to your presentation. You want to thrill your audience and the event planner.

Not only can you overdeliver in your presentation, you can give your audience a bonus at the end of your presentation.

This bonus can be a PDF copy of your recent book. It can be a free half-hour consultation with you on the phone. It can be access to your free weekly newsletter. It can be anything that is pertinent to your presentation and gives your audience tangible benefit relevant to why they came to your presentation in the first place.

***

Now you know practicing ten thousand hours, giving your audience what they want and need, and amazing and delighting them by overdelivering more than what they expect will place you in the upper echelon of speakers.

Every great speaker started out as a not-so-great speaker. However, if you seek out speaking opportunities frequently and continuously improve on your last speaking performance, you will one day step into the elite group of speakers who delight, amaze, and astound their audiences.

It is not a matter of if. It is a matter of when!

CALL TO ACTION

- Speak as often as you can on your way to ten thousand hours of practice.
- For your next and all subsequent presentations, spend the required time to determine what your audience wants and needs.
- Delight, amaze, and astound your audience in all future presentations by giving them more than they paid for.

"A talk is a voyage with purpose, and it must be charted. The man who starts out going nowhere generally gets there."

—Dale Carnegie

PART IV: PRESENTATION DELIVERY

THERE ARE TWO PARTS you need to master if you are going to deliver great presentations. They are your presentation preparation (Parts II and III of this book) and your presentation delivery (covered in Part IV here).

Please realize that your delivery is your presentation to your audience. You may think your slides, your videos, your exercises that you used in your presentation preparation are your presentation. You would be mistaken if this is what you think. Your audience is not privy to your slides, videos, exercises, and your presentation practice.

Part IV covers the following topics:

- Dress for Success!
- The "Eyes" Have It!
- Do You Talk with Your Hands?
- Don't Fall into the "Apology Trap!"

- The Question and Answer Period: UGH!
- When Things Go Wrong in Your Presentation!
- Great Listening = Great Speaking!
- Are You Credible to Your Audience?
- You Are Your Presentation!
- Are Your Intentions Known?

DRESS FOR SUCCESS!

"What you wear is how you present yourself to the world, especially today, when human contacts are so quick. Fashion is instant language."
— Miuccia Prada

FAR BE IT FROM me to describe myself as a fashion maven. But over the years being in the business world, I have learned a thing or two past the common fashion errors such as wearing socks of different colors, belt and shoes of a different color, and shirt and blazer of different colors not appropriate together, such as a yellow shirt with a navy-blue suit.

For this chapter, we are going to take a public speaker fashion journey to explore speaking attire appropriate to your audience, venue, and topic; the colors that evoke the audience response you want; and, finally, speaking attire don'ts.

APPROPRIATENESS TO THE AUDIENCE, VENUE, AND TOPIC

Whether you like it or not, your audience is forming their first impression of you purely by the way you look. It may not be fair, but it is reality. It is important you wear clothes that are appropriate for the audience, venue, and topic.

I attended the National Speakers Association Influence 2019. There was another smaller convention of the National Cattlemen's Association at the venue. I saw a lot of people wearing cowboy and cowgirl hats. In the case of the National Cattlemen's Association convention, it would be entirely appropriate for the speakers to wear cowboy or cowgirl hats. It would be entirely inappropriate for a speaker at the Influence 2019 convention to wear a cowboy or cowgirl hat unless his or her presentation related to cowboys and/or cowgirls. It is important you dress as your audience does.

If you are a man and the men in your audience are wearing sports jackets with open collars, as a speaker, you should wear a sports jacket with a tie or a suit with a tie. If you are a woman and some of the women in your audience are wearing pants while others are wearing skirts or dresses, I recommend you wear a dress. Always dress one step up from your audience. This will add to your authority as the speaker.

Wearing clothes that somewhat mirror what your audience is wearing draws the audience to you.

Matching your speaking attire to the venue is easy. The earlier in the day your presentation is, the more informal you can be.

If you are speaking at the opening morning plenary session at a conference, a sports jacket and open collar for men and a smart-looking pantsuit or nice blouse with a skirt for women is entirely appropriate. At a morning plenary session, you are trying to get the audience excited about the day to come. Informality in your attire will relax the audience and make them look forward to the day's presentations.

At Influence 2019, one of the speakers at the opening afternoon plenary session was Erik Weihenmayer, the first blind person to reach the summit of Mount Everest. His talk was truly inspiring. He had on a flannel shirt, jeans, and hiking boots. This was a great example of how your dress when you are speaking is appropriate to the topic. If he wore a suit and tie while talking about how he scaled Mount Everest, he would have completely lost the audience. When your attire does not match your topic, there is a good chance the audience won't trust what you are saying.

If you are speaking at a luncheon, for men a business suit or even a sports jacket, dress slacks, and a tie would be appropriate. If you are a woman, a dress would be appropriate.

If you are speaking at a formal dinner at night, wear a dark suit and a tie if you are a man and wear a subdued cocktail dress or long gown if you are a woman.

Avoid wearing provocative clothing when you speak. Your audience will be distracted and may be insulted. You don't want anything to distract the audience from your message.

What you wear when you speak should be appropriate to the audience, venue, and topic. You now know what to wear. So what colors are the most appropriate?

COLORS THAT EVOKE THE AUDIENCE RESPONSE YOU WANT

The following information on colors to wear when you are speaking is from "These are the Best Colors to Wear While Presenting" (www.presentationtraininginstitute.com/these-are-the-best-colors-to-wear-while-presenting/):

- *Dress for Power*. "Deep, dark colors tend to exude power more than bright colors. So, if you want to come across as an intelligent, credible presenter stick with dark colors such as black, charcoal, deep taupe, grey, or dark blue. These colors are heavier and come across as more authoritative. They are an ideal choice for formal presentations about analytical topics."

- *Excite your audience*. "It might be that you are plugging a new product and therefore want to grab the attention of your audience. If you are giving a presentation that is a little less formal and more upbeat, you want to wear a color that will reach out and grab the audience's attention. Red has been shown to increase heart rates and excite an audience. Yellow is another attention grabber and it is great for stimulating mental activity and retaining attention. Purple is often perceived as a luxurious color that can boost creativity. These brighter hues are great for presentations that are meant to excite and persuade audiences."

- **Build Trust and Confidence.** "Sometimes the purpose of a presentation is to inform an audience. In an informative presentation it is important to build trust and rapport with the audience. Blue is often a calming color and has been associated with tranquility and trust. Green can also be perceived as warm and nurturing, because it reminds us of nature. Grey is the most neutral and can work well in informative presentations as well."

I have explained that what you should wear when you speak should be appropriate to the audience, venue, and topic. I have also talked about what the best colors are to wear in different situations. I have covered the do's of speaking attire. Finally, I will talk about what not to wear when you are speaking.

SPEAKING ATTIRE DON'TS

The following information on what not to wear when you are presenting was adapted from "How To Avoid Disaster: Six Rules For What To Wear When Giving A Speech" by Nick Morgan (https://www.forbes. com/sites/nickmorgan/2013/12/05/how-to-avoid-disaster-six-rules-for-what-to-wear-when-giving-a-speech/#430d63afc1ef). Below are six don'ts when it comes to speaking attire:

- **Don't dress *slightly worse* than the audience**. Your audience has come to hear an impressive person speak. They have not come to hear a person like the person next to them at the bar. Think subdued star power when you dress.
- **Don't dress consistently with your brand**. This is an error that far too many speakers make. If your brand is the outdoors, by all means, wear jeans and boots and a flannel shirt. If you're a creative type, wear something that signals that. If you're a boring banker, then wear a gray suit.
- **Don't dress to feel like a five-dollar bill**. Your audiences will be as enthusiastic about your subject as much as you. So you want to "ooze" with enthusiasm. A prerequisite of enthusiasm is being confident in yourself. A prerequisite of being confident in yourself is to look good. When you look good, you feel good. When you feel good, you will deliver your most powerful presentations. Dress so you feel like a million bucks.
- **Don't dress in clothing that restricts your movement**. To take advantage of your full repertoire of gestures, you must have unrestricted access to move your hands and your body in whatever ways make your presentations more meaningful. When you speak, wear comfortable-fitting clothes to facilitate maximum ability to gesticulate and move your body to the rhythms of your presentation.
- **Don't dress in clothing that is meant for someone twenty years younger than you**. Have you ever seen the man or woman who speaks in clothing meant for someone twenty years younger? I have. The audience cringing comes to mind. Whether the speaker is a sixty-year-old man with an open collar and gold chains or a fifty-five-year-old woman with a short skirt and flashy

jewelry, the incongruity of their attire and their age will greatly distract the audience. Always wear clothing that is appropriate to your age. You and your audience will be glad you did.

- **Don't dress so you will blend into the audience.** I previously mentioned audiences come to see a super star speaker. So be the super star the audience wants. Wear the sharp business suit if you are a man or a power pantsuit if you are a woman. Remember, the audience is coming to hear the expert in the topic. Dress like the expert.

We took a public speaker fashion journey to explore speaking attire appropriate to your audience, venue, and topic; colors that evoke the audience response you want; and, finally, speaking attire don'ts.

Wear the right clothes when you speak, and you will immeasurably add to your influence with your audiences!

CALL TO ACTION

- Wear attire appropriate to the audience, venue, and presentation topic.
- Wear colors that evoke the audience response you want.
- Observe the six speaking attire don'ts earlier in this chapter.

"Fashion is a tool. . . to compete in life outside the home. People like you better, without knowing why, because people always react well to a person they like the looks of."

—Mary Quant

THE "EYES" HAVE IT!

*"Great speakers find a way of making an early
connection with their audience. It can be as simple as
walking confidently on stage, looking around, making
eye contact with two or three people, and smiling."*
—Chris Anderson, TED Talks curator

NO SOLDIER WOULD GO ill-equipped into battle. Nor should you give a presentation without your full complement of presentation delivery equipment in good working order. Beginning speakers often overlook this.

So, what is your full complement of presentation delivery equipment? You have your voice with all the variety it brings. You have the way you look, which has more effect on your presentation than you think. You also have your body language, which conveys the most communication to your audience. Believe it or not!

In this chapter, we will concentrate on one of the most important parts of your body language: eye contact.

Great eye contact builds rapport with your audience, shows and builds your confidence, and treats the audience with respect. Read on to learn why.

GOOD EYE CONTACT BUILDS RAPPORT WITH YOUR AUDIENCE

 The value of good eye contact is easy to prove. Remember the last conversation you had with a friend or acquaintance when the other person was not looking at you while he or she was talking? How did this make you feel? There is a better than even chance you felt that the person was not listening to you, or that he or she didn't think you were important enough to look in the eye, or that he or she did not really want to connect with you.

When you avoid eye contact with your audience, you cause the formation of the same thoughts in audience members' minds. As I mentioned above, eye contact is a powerful part of your presentation delivery equipment. You should use it to build rapport with your audience. So how do you use eye contact to build rapport with your audience?

You can start before the presentation gets underway. Get to your presentation's venue at least an hour before the presentation. If you are not the first presentation, get to the venue an hour before the first presentation. Mix with the audience and ask them questions about them; don't make statements about yourself.

Think back to kindergarten and how you made friends there. Start with, "My name is _____. What's yours?" Look audience members in the eye and show true interest in who they are, why they came, and what they hope to take away and use from your presentation.

The most interesting people at cocktail parties, weddings, or at your presentations are not the people you know; they are the people you don't know. Introducing yourself to audience members before your presentation and making eye contact with them is a winning combination to build rapport with your audience.

So, great eye contact builds rapport with your audience. Another great benefit of great eye contact both before, during, and after your presentation is it increases your confidence about your subject matter and your ability to convey it to your audience.

GREAT EYE CONTACT SHOWS CONFIDENCE

 Great eye contact increases your confidence, because you can actually feel the audience connecting. What is a greater reward for you as a public speaker than to get through to your audience?

Positive audience reaction actually gives you confidence. Number one, you know they are listening. Number two, their positive reaction gives you the indication that they are, if not agreeing with you, at least "in tune" with what you are saying. Number three, there is no greater need of humans than to be understood. (There's that rule of three again.)

Author Steven Covey's fifth habit of highly effective people is, "Seek first to understand, then to be understood." Why is this? You and all other people have a craving to be understood by others. This understanding by the audience of what you are saying will encourage you to speak with confidence and authority. Believe it or not, you will find yourself enjoying speaking to your audience, and this, also, will give you confidence.

Your great eye contact has built rapport with your audience and you are gaining confidence because of their positive reactions and you know the audience is getting your points. There is another benefit for your great eye contact.

GREAT EYE CONTACT SHOWS RESPECT

When I was growing up, my father had this preoccupation with respect—respect for him and my mom, respect for my friends, and respect for myself. What is this thing about respect that is so important and will draw you closer to your audience?

Showing respect to your audience means they feel they are in a safe place where they will be able to express themselves when the question and answer period arrives. Respect for your audience also will build the audience's trust in you. Your audience will trust you to tell the truth, properly attribute material not your own, and accept their opinion even if you don't share it.

Be fair in your treatment of your material. You can only look at the headlines of today to prove there is much division in this world mostly caused by both sides of an issue not respecting the other side's opinion. Try presenting both sides in your next presentation and then let your audience decide which side won.

In his law career, Lincoln used the technique of arguing his opponent's side as well as his own side. However, he was able to subtly hint that his side was best. Because of this and other traits, he was nicknamed Honest Abe and won many cases. When you present both sides of an issue, you respect your audience and gain much respect yourself from the audience.

***

Great eye contact builds rapport with your audience, builds your confidence, and shows respect to the audience members, drawing them closer to you as a speaker.

No doubt you have other reasons that come to your mind about the importance of good eye contact. I invite you to send me your reasons at frank@speakleadandsucceed.com. Please let me know if I can use your thoughts in a future book.

Remember, the eyes have it!

CALL TO ACTION

- Use great eye contact to build rapport with your audience.
- Use great eye contact to build and show your confidence.
- Use great eye contact to show respect to your audience.

"Eye contact is often one of the most overlooked methods we have to connect, build rapport, and be effective as a speaker and leader."

—Joseph Guarino,
professional speaker and trainer

DO YOU TALK WITH YOUR HANDS?

"Hand gestures are really a powerful aspect of communication, from both the speaker's and the listener's end."
—Dr. Carol Kinsey Goman, body language expert and author of *The Nonverbal Advantage: Secrets and Science of Body Language at Work* and *The Silent Language of Leaders*

HAVE YOU EVER TALKED to a friend on the street? When you were talking, what were your hands doing? Were they at your side stationary or were they moving around in front of you synchronized to what you were saying? My guess is they were doing the latter.

When I consult with my clients about their public speaking, gestures are a major part of this consultation. Why? Because gestures are a vital part of your presentation equipment. If you don't use gestures, you are missing out on a great way to add much more to your private and public speaking.

In this chapter, we will explore why gestures are most effective when they are spontaneous, why gestures draw your audiences toward you, and how gestures enhance the words you are speaking.

SPONTANEOUS GESTURES ARE TRUSTED BY THE AUDIENCE

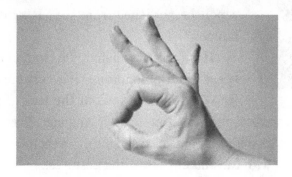

Some people look at gestures as another language. In a way, it is. American Sign Language (ASL) is an example using your hands to convey communication. But I am not talking about ASL. I am talking about gestures that are used to enhance and emphasize your speaking.

The most effective and most trusted gestures are spontaneous. What I mean by "spontaneous gestures" is gestures that magically appear when you are speaking. You don't have to consciously think about them. They are just there conveying more information.

Now, if we just stay with the gestures that are spontaneous to us, we would be missing out on a large part of the gestures available to us.

This may sound contradictory, but gestures can be practiced until they are spontaneous.

So how do spontaneous gestures draw your audience toward you?

GESTURES DRAW YOUR AUDIENCE TOWARD YOU

Gestures can either draw an audience to you or repel the audience from you. How does this happen?

Have you ever listened to someone who is speaking in a monotone? It is very boring, isn't it? Well, you can look at the lack of gestures when you speak as the monotone of body language. Even a person speaking with a modulated voice can improve their delivery and connection with the audience by using gestures.

Open gestures like holding your arms out to full length and opening the palms of your hands are best because they draw the audience toward you. Closed gestures like folding your arms on your chest or holding your hands together push the audience away from you.

If you mention a series of items when you are speaking, consider holding up fingers to indicate number in the sequence to which you are referring.

Also, ensure that your gestures match what you are saying. When they do, they will make it easier for the audience to see your point. When they don't match the words you are saying, it is confusing for the audience. In fact, some audience members may actually tune out your presentation.

We know that spontaneous gestures are trusted by your audiences and gestures draw your audiences toward you. So how do gestures actually enhance the words you are speaking?

GESTURES ENHANCE THE WORDS YOU ARE SPEAKING

Here are a few examples of how gestures can enhance the words you are speaking.

Suppose you come to a part of your presentation when you need to indicate something strong. If your gestures were a clenched fist or even two clenched fists, these gestures would enhance your presentation. You could even hold up your arm and make a muscle, which would indicate strength if that is what your words say.

If you needed to indicate the whole audience in your presentation, you could open your arms to the audience. You could also sweep one or both hands across the audience.

If you needed to show sadness in your presentation, you could fold your hands in a reverent way. You could also open your arms to the audience but lower as in almost pointing down.

I could go on and on with examples, but I will stop with these three. In the first section above, I mentioned gestures that are spontaneous are the most trusted by the audience. So how do you get the right gestures into your presentation if they are not spontaneous? You can actually make new gestures spontaneous by practicing them in front of a mirror. In fact, before you practice a presentation in front of people, always practice it in front of a mirror first. You will be surprised by what you see.

***

We have explored why gestures are most effective when they are spontaneous, why gestures draw your audiences toward you, and how gestures enhance the words you are speaking.

One final thought in paraphrasing Thomas Jefferson, "If you want to do something you have never done, you have to become someone you have never been."

Thinking about these words in relation to gestures, you may not readily use gestures when you speak. If you don't, you are missing out on a great way to connect with your audience. I believe you can learn to use any new gesture and go a long way in drawing your audiences toward you.

CALL TO ACTION

- Use spontaneous gestures to gain your audience's trust.
- Use gestures to draw your audience toward you.
- Use gestures to enhance the words you are speaking.

"Research demonstrates that the movements we make with our hands when we talk constitute a kind of second language, adding information that is absent from our words."

—Annie Murphy Paul, author of Brilliant: The New Science of Smart as told in Business Insider

DON'T FALL INTO THE "APOLOGY TRAP!"

"Designing a presentation without an audience in mind is like writing a love letter and addressing it 'to whom it may concern.'"

—Ken Haemer

"OH, I HAVE LOST my place." "Sorry, I missed a whole section of my talk." "Someone must have shuffled my notes."

Have you ever heard a speaker apologize like this? What did you think, how did you feel, and how did you react when this happened? Did you think, "Boy, is this apologizing by the speaker distracting!" Did you feel uncomfortable the speaker was having a hard time with his/her presentation? Did you feel angry with the speaker for wasting your time?

If you have never heard a speaker apologize like this in his/her presentation, get ready. In the near future, there is a good chance you will hear these apologies from a speaker near you!

In their book, *Present Like a Pro*, Cyndi Maxey and Kevin O'Connor tells us not to fall into the Apology Trap. They also talk about the consequences if you do. Some of the following information is adapted from *Present Like a Pro*.

There are three important reasons why you should never apologize during your presentation: (1) you will lose credibility for your topic, (2) you will distract the audience from your message, and (3) you will alert and probably annoy the audience with things they don't care about.

LOSING CREDIBILITY FOR YOUR TOPIC

Remember the boy or girl in high school that always apologized for himself or herself and sometimes for others? Did you respect this boy or girl? My guess is you did not. Maybe at the time you thought the person was a little weird and then, with age, you just felt sorry for him/her. Thoughts of his/her insecurity probably passed through your mind then as they may now.

Now picture you as a speaker apologizing in your presentation opening and/or body and/or closing. Would the confidence of the audience in you suffer? I know it would for me.

People come to see and hear you speak because they view you as the expert on your subject. They have come to learn from you. But apologizing during your presentation has the opposite effect from what you want: the audience disengages, is annoyed with you for wasting their time, and is very uncomfortable with you fumbling through your presentation.

On the rare occasion when your audience does notice something has gone wrong in your presentation, here is your opportunity to shine. You can actually increase your credibility as a speaker in your audience's eyes by handling the mishap as they think a professional speaker should. Control your nervousness about the situation. People in control are admired by others. You will be admired by your audience if you simply move on righting the faux pas as best as possible. If this is not possible, you will have "Plan B" and "Plan C" ready, if necessary.

One reason not to apologize during your presentation is that you will lose credibility with your audience. You will also distract the audience from your message.

DISTRACTING THE AUDIENCE FROM YOUR MESSAGE

The most important goal of your presentation is to communicate your message to your audience effectively and persuasively. Apologizing during your presentation distracts the audience from your message.

I tell my public speaking clients their audience does not know when you have made a mistake until you point it out to them. So when something goes wrong in your presentation, and it will, resist the urge to point out the errors you have made.

I was witness to a presentation at my local National Speakers Association chapter meeting that was a great illustration of what to do when something goes wrong in your presentation. The computer that was projecting slides went blank. So what did the speaker do? Did he complain about it? Did he apologize to the audience for the problem? Did he stumble and falter over his words? He did nothing of the kind. When the computer went blank, he immediately gave us a small group exercise (his Plan B), which afforded the time to fix the blank screen problem.

When military special forces train, they rehearse over and over and over again all the things that can go wrong in a military operation and their response in all these situations.

List the situations that can arise in your presentations: blank screen, you slip and fall down, your notes are out of order, etc. If you rehearse what you would do in these situations, you will know what action you need to take to minimize or eliminate the damage. At the very least, chances are the audience will not even know something has gone wrong.

You now know that apologizing in your presentation decreases your credibility and distracts your audience from your message. If you apologize during your presentation, you will also alert your audience to things they don't care about.

ALERTING YOUR AUDIENCE TO THINGS THEY DON'T CARE ABOUT

In the words of Cyndi Maxey and Kevin O'Connor in *Present Like a Pro*, when things go wrong in your presentation, "It's your problem, not theirs." Don't look for sympathy, acknowledgment, or solutions from the audience. The problem with your presentation delivery is yours and only yours to solve.

The audience does not care about the problems in your presentation. They only care about what is in it for them. What can they learn? Do they feel better leaving the presentation than they did when they came? What more can they learn from the speaker?

Apologizing for problems in your presentation adds unnecessary information that muddles your message. You want the audience to get your message as easy as adding two and two.

You also run better than even odds you will annoy some or maybe even a majority of your audience. Ask yourself how hard is it to influence an audience that is annoyed with you. The answer is it is practically impossible.

Don't distract the audience away from your message and toward the errors in your presentation.

***

We have covered three important reasons why you should never apologize during your presentation. They are (1) you will lose credibility, (2) you will distract the audience from your message, and (3) you will alert the audience to things they basically don't care about.

So now you know.

Don't fall into the apology trap!

CALL TO ACTION

- Retain your credibility with your audience by not apologizing.
- Retain your audience's attention by not pointing out things that did not go according to your plan.
- Don't alert your audience to things they don't care about by apologizing.

"They may forget what you said, but they will never forget how you made them feel."

—Carl W. Buechner

THE QUESTION AND ANSWER PERIOD: UGH!

"Oratory is the power to talk people out of their sober and natural opinions."

—Joseph Chatfield

JOSEPH CHATFIELD HAD IT right. The purpose of your presentations is to convince the audience to share your opinion of your subject, especially if at the beginning of your presentation, they did not hold your opinion of your subject.

When you have stopped talking, the presentation is not done. Inevitably, there is a question and answer (Q&A) period after your presentations. The Q&A period is also part of the presentation. The only difference is for the talking part of your presentation, you knew what you would say. In the Q&A period, you don't know what the audience's questions will be. Or do you?

Below are three Q&A situations and how to deal with them.

HOW YOU SHOULD FIELD HOSTILE QUESTIONS

Handling hostile questions is always tough. You may have someone in the audience that, despite your cogent arguments to the contrary, still does not agree with you. This doesn't make their questions hostile. When I say hostile, what I mean is an arrogant questioner, interrupting you, and asking their question in an arrogant, sarcastic, or condescending way. So what do you do?

Never respond in kind to a hostile questioner. Remember, the hostile questioner is still part of the audience. A good way (don't do this) to create a hostile audience is to be hostile yourself as the speaker. If you "take the high road," the audience will eventually self-correct a hostile questioner.

Another method to use with a hostile questioner is for you to say something like, "You seem passionate about your opinion, and I respect that. My answer to your question will take more time than I have right now. Would you agree to see me at the break so I can give you a more complete answer?"

There are times, and they are rare, where the above two methods do not work. Tell the hostile questioner you will see them at the break and take another question even if the hostile questioner is still asking their question. The audience will usually start booing the hostile questioner and tell them to be quiet.

So above are some methods to handle the hostile questioner, but what if you do not know the answer to a question?

WHAT YOU SHOULD DO WHEN YOU DON'T KNOW THE ANSWER TO A QUESTION

When I was a kid, there were a few times where I told a "white lie," mostly to get out of punishment from my parents. I learned from this experience that if you tell a lie, you have to maintain the lie. Also, the lie may grow to something bigger and then you have to maintain the bigger lie. Pay me now or pay me later. The price is always cheaper if you tell the truth. It is the same with answering a question from the audience.

If you do not know the answer to a question, don't "beat around the bush." State quickly and emphatically that you do not know the answer to the question, but if the questioner sees you at the break, you can get their e-mail address and get them an answer within a day.

If you try to answer an audience question when you don't know the answer, it will become evident quickly to the audience that you don't.

Although not sufficient to giving an outstanding presentation, establishment and maintenance of your credibility with your audience is absolutely essential. With it, you have the opportunity to really change people's lives. Without it, you don't have a prayer of doing this.

Getting a question from the audience that you can't answer will throw you off initially. Another type of audience question will also: the question unrelated to your topic.

HOW YOU SHOULD FIELD A QUESTION UNRELATED TO YOUR TOPIC

Although not common, occasionally you will get a question from an audience member that is slightly or grossly unrelated to your topic. This type of question can be tricky to answer. You don't want to embarrass the audience member. Embarrassing audience members is a killer to your likability to the audience. Don't do it under any circumstances even if you are embarrassed or annoyed by the question. Let's run through some scenarios.

Suppose you are presenting a new space orbital theory at the national convention in your industry. An audience member asks you the following question: "How does your theory affect climate change?" Now in your presentation, you did not talk about climate change, but you can see how someone who is concerned about climate change may think that the orbital path of the planets in our solar system might be related to climate change. How should you answer?

You could say, "My presentation did not remotely mention climate change, so I am going to have to move on to the next question." After this answer, you would alienate a good portion of the audience because you would be dismissing the question of an audience member. Here is a better response: "I can see how you would bring in climate change." This validates the question and brings you closer to the audience.

You could go on to say, "Climate change is an area I have read about, but I am certainly not an expert in the area. Perhaps at the break, we could meet so I can learn more of your concerns about climate change and give you my best answer to your question." What have you done here? You have affirmed the validity of the question and given the audience questioner a golden opportunity to get a more complete answer from you. You both win.

Suppose you are presenting your doctoral thesis concerning a new radar signal processing algorithm you developed. You get the following question from the audience: "Does your signal processing algorithm work for communication signals also?"

No doubt there are similarities between radar signal processing and communications signal processing, but going into the communications signal processing area would dilute your main points. You might respond, "Thanks for that interesting question. I have been concentrating on radar signal processing. I will have to do a bit of research and consult with some colleagues to see if my algorithm applies to communications signal processing. Please see me after the presentation to give me your e-mail address. I will get back to you."

So, what have you done here? Again, you have validated the question (always a good thing) and have made plans on the spot to get back to the audience questioner. Good stuff.

Questions unrelated to your topic will pop up every now and then. During your presentation preparation, it would be good if you practiced answers to unrelated questions so you will know how to answer them before you are asked in a live presentation.

***

The question and answer period of your presentation can be a very stressful time for you. However, if you practice fielding (1) hostile questions, (2) questions to which you don't know the answer, and (3) questions unrelated to your topic, you will be well on your way to answering audience questions in a cogent, concise, and confident manner.

CALL TO ACTION

- Take the "high road" with the hostile questioner; the audience will self-correct the hostile questioner.
- When you do not know the answer to a question, admit this quickly and tell the questioner if he or she sees you at the break, you can get their e-mail address and send them an answer within twenty-four hours.
- Field a question that is unrelated to your topic by telling the questioner to please see you about the question on the break.

"According to most studies, people's number one fear is public speaking. Number two is death. Death is number two. Does that sound right? This means to the average person, if you go to a funeral, you're better off in the casket than doing the eulogy."

—Jerry Seinfeld

WHEN THINGS GO WRONG IN YOUR PRESENTATION!

"Many attempts to communicate are nullified by saying too much."

—Robert Greenleaf

WE ALL HAVE TO perform sometime in our lives. Whether it is a presentation, the school spelling bee, the high jump, or a million other possible things, we are not perfect. Because we are not perfect, we will have problems in our performances from time to time.

There is a great saying I heard, "It is not how far you fall. It is how high you bounce." Can you use this sentiment in your presentations and other areas of your life? You bet you can!

Below we will discuss what you do when things go wrong in your presentation, but realize that the words below pertain to driving a car, singing the solo in your church's choir, or asking the love of your life to marry you!

REMAIN CALM

I remember a T-shirt that was given to my daughter and the other musicians in her elementary school band. The T-Shirt said, "Remain Calm and Play On!" What a great saying. When you encounter problems in your presentation, do you remain calm and carry on? If you do, you are in a small minority.

One of my mentors from his audio programs, Earl Nightingale, says, "Fully 92 percent of worries are about things that happened in the past we have no control over or things that never happen." Believe it or not!

Now certainly, problems can occur in your presentation, but the vast majority of them will not be noticed by your audience until you tell them. So don't tell them!

As I mentioned previously in the chapter entitled, "Don't Fall Into the Apology Trap," the propensity presenters have is for apologizing for a faux pas in their presentation. You, as a speaker, have no obligation to point out the problems in your presentation. In fact, the hard truth is your audience does not care about the problems in your presentation.

I give a seminar on child sexual abuse awareness and prevention two to three times a year. I encountered a circumstance one time in a session that would throw most speakers. The seminar started at nine a.m. I am usually there by eight a.m. to set up the room and review my notes. When I arrived at the venue, I discovered the room was mistakenly booked and would not be open until eight forty-five a.m. I also noticed the meeting room for the previous meeting was set up with tables in a U-shaped configuration. I usually have audience seating with chairs in rows and an aisle down the center. I assured the sponsor we could work something out. I thought, let's keep the configuration the way it is. It will stimulate more discussion. The audience was clueless that I don't usually have the configuration in U-shaped form. The session turned out to be one of the best sessions I have ever had.

Panicking actually retards your thinking process. When you remain calm, your tendency will be to think of solutions and not the problem.

Try this. When a problem occurs in your presentation, first pause, take a deep breath, and then remember how you planned to recover in your preparation for your presentation. More on this in the next section.

PRACTICE RECOVERY BEFORE YOUR PRESENTATION

When I was in the U.S. Air Force, we had a saying, "We train the way we fight and fight the way we train." Have you seen the movie *Top Gun* with Tom Cruise? You may remember the aerial dogfight scenes. They were pretty realistic. Think about the reactions pilots have to have to fly safely, perform their mission, and then return to base safely. Prior to any mission, pilots practice what can go wrong and how they will react to the situation. We as speakers need to do the same.

When colonels and generals plan a battle, they think of everything that could happen and what their response will be if it does not. In other words, in war games or, at least, on paper, they have thought of every mishap that can happen and have a response for each and every mishap.

Now what does *Top Gun* and going into battle have to do with your presentations? It has everything to do with your presentations. The lesson from the last two paragraphs is for you to think of all the things that can go wrong during your presentation and what you will do when they happen. It is great to think about your responses to problems, but it is even better to play act them out during your presentation. This is the whole reason for the U.S. Navy's *Top Gun* and the U.S. Air Force's Fighter Weapons schools.

So, what can go wrong? Well, for one, your computer with your slides may go kaput. What will you do if you have no visuals? One thing you can do is go right into a group exercise, which will give you time to recover from the blank computer.

The microphone may not work, and you will have to shout out your presentation so the guy in the last row can hear you. What will you do? Maybe you will go into the center of the audience and do your presentation from there so you won't have to shout as loud.

Finally, there are many more things that can go wrong. What if you have a terrible cold that has settled into your larynx and you can barely speak? What will you do? Ensure a microphone is available and working so you don't have to try to shout.

It is better to think and play act all these mishaps before your presentation to prepare responses to them.

We have talked about staying calm during problems with your presentation. Remember, the audience doesn't know there has been a mishap, and if they did, they would not care about it. We have also talked about practicing recovery from presentation mishaps during your preparation for your presentation.

Let's now talk about what to do in the unlikely, but possible, occurrence when your audience realizes there is a problem in your presentation.

IN THE RARE CASE WHERE YOUR AUDIENCE DISCOVERS THE PROBLEM

I was attending a National Speakers Association Washington, DC Chapter meeting a number of months ago and was listening to a great speaker when his computer projection went blank. This problem could not be covered up. So what do you think the speaker did? He immediately gave us an appropriate exercise to do, which gave him the time to fix the computer projection problem.

Do you think the speaker on the spur of the moment thought to give us an exercise? No. That exercise was planned for a mishap, in this case, the computer projection going blank.

If you are witty and the audience notices the problem, you may even make a joke about it like, "The screen was too bright for me anyway. I needed some blank screen time." Okay, so it sounds corny, but corny is okay with most audiences. At least it gets them laughing and enjoying themselves. I will take audiences enjoying themselves any day.

If you are into corny jokes, you may want to say, "For those who don't like corny jokes, it is my policy to keep saying them until I get maximum applause." If this doesn't get you rousing applause, I don't know what will.

My main point here is there are many ways to recover from a problem in your presentation noticed by the audience. One of the best ways is humor. Humor about yourself is the most prized by audiences. Humor about others will get you indignation from your audience and no referrals from them.

***

So what have we learned today?

We learned if you "Remain Calm and Play On" you will recover and have a good if not great performance.

We also learned if you plan recoveries to the possible mishaps in your presentations, you will instinctively invoke the backup plan when bad things happen in your presentations.

Finally, you learned some techniques on how to recover when the audience does know there is a problem in your presentation.

When things go wrong in your presentation, be confident to know you have already rehearsed your recovery!

CALL TO ACTION

- Remain calm when things go wrong in your presentation; a calm mind generates thinking power.
- Devise plans to handle everything that could possibly go wrong in your presentation before you deliver your presentation.
- In the rare case where you audience discovers what has gone wrong in your presentation, tell them what your previously created plan is to recover.

"If you can't explain it simply, you don't understand it well enough."

—Albert Einstein

GREAT LISTENING = GREAT SPEAKING!

"Listen with curiosity. Speak with honesty. Act with integrity. The greatest problem with communication is we don't listen to understand. We listen to reply. When we listen with curiosity, we don't listen with the intent to reply. We listen for what's behind the words."
—Roy T. Bennett, The Light in the Heart

IT'S IRONIC, BUT USING your listening skills actually makes you a better speaker. One of the best ways to improve your public speaking ability is by listening to those who have the knowledge you need.

Below are three ways you can use your listening skills to become a better speaker.

ENGAGE AND LISTEN TO YOUR AUDIENCE BEFORE YOUR PRESENTATION

How can you hope to achieve the goal of your presentation without having the foggiest idea of what your audience knows and feels about your topic?

There are three ways to determine what your audience knows and feels about your topic. The best way is to talk to your audience's members before your presentation. The second-best way is to talk to others who know what members of your audience know and feel about your topic. The third-best way is to read what audience members have said about your topic, including their writings and videos.

When you talk to members of the audience or those who know members of the audience, use active listening skills. By active listening skills, I mean to ask clarifying questions. As Stephen Covey says, "Seek to understand, then to be understood."

If you cannot ask questions of audience members or those who know audience members, seek out what audience members have written on your topic, including videos.

Use the added knowledge you learn to more completely prepare your presentation. Use discovered objections to your topic to develop counterarguments to these objections.

Active listening skills are vitally important to determine what your audience is thinking on your topic. It also has application in gaining knowledge during practice presentation evaluations before the presentation.

LISTEN TO AND IMPLEMENT PRE-PRESENTATION EVALUATION SUGGESTIONS

It is of great importance to practice your delivery in front of trusted colleagues and friends before the actual presentation. Their written feedback is extremely valuable because you have documentation of the great parts of your presentation and areas where you can improve.

Verbal feedback is particularly useful. With verbal feedback, you get the advantage of additional communication through the evaluator's body language and tone of voice.

When listening to your colleagues and friends evaluate your presentation, tune out any other thoughts except what the evaluator is saying. Use your active listening skills (asking questions about what your evaluator is saying) to further understand the intent of the evaluator.

Your active listening skills also have application during the question and answer session of your presentation.

LISTEN TO AUDIENCE QUESTIONS AND ANSWER THEM MORE CONFIDENTLY

 How many of you have listened to a speaker answer an audience question and in the back of your mind a little voice is saying, "He/she did not really answer the question?"

There are a number of reasons why this may happen during your presentations. Some reasons are (1) you may be nervous and answer a different question, (2) you may have misinterpreted the question, and (3) you do not know the answer to the question but feel you must answer it intelligently or you will lose credibility with the audience.

Here are a few ways to solve this:

First, repeat the question for the audience. Very often, others in the audience cannot hear the question. Repeating the question "tunes" the audience in to the question. An added benefit is it gives you time to think of a cogent answer.

Second, as in the previous section, use your active listening (asking questions about the audience member's question) to further understand the questioner's intent.

Third, when you think you have finished answering the question, always ask the questioner, "Have I fully answered your question?" If you have, great. If you haven't, and there is time, ask the questioner what part of the question you have left unanswered and then answer that part. If there is not time to re-answer the question, politely ask the questioner to see you after the presentation.

So, to become a better speaker:

- Listen to what your audience says before the presentation.
- Listen to and implement pre-presentation evaluation suggestions.
- Listen to audience questions and answer them more confidently.

Remember, we learn much more when we listen than when we talk. Hone your listening skills and you will greatly improve your speaking ability.

CALL TO ACTION

- Engage and listen to your audience beforehand to discover their expertise on your presentation's subject, their opinion of your subject, and advocates of your subject.
- Modify your presentation according to what you find out about the audience prior to your presentation.
- Concerning audience questions, seek to understand the question before you even think about your response.

"Most of the successful people I've known are the ones who do more listening than talking."

—Bernard Baruch

ARE YOU CREDIBLE TO YOUR AUDIENCE?

"In the end, you make your reputation and you have your success based upon credibility and being able to provide people who are really hungry for information what they want."

—Brit Hume

YOU ALL KNOW THAT your job credibility is key in determining your salary, your level of responsibility, and your reputation in your company.

How valuable would it be to you if I were to show you how to increase your credibility? Plenty, I imagine.

In this chapter, I will give you three fundamental ways to increase your credibility in front of your audiences. They are (1) know the level of your audience on your subject, (2) increase your influence with your audience through positive body language, and (3) become an expert at answering audience questions.

KNOW THE LEVEL OF YOUR AUDIENCE ON YOUR SUBJECT

It is important to know at what level your audience is on your subject. Now why is this important? For one very good reason: you can then adjust the level of the presentation for this particular audience. You don't want to waste your time presenting information the audience already knows.

The best way to determine what level your audience is at is to seek their feedback before the presentation. In addition to determining the level of your audience on your presentation subject, it also gives you the opportunity to determine any contrarian views to what you are presenting, which allows you to incorporate items in your presentation that answer these contrarian views. Feedback prior to your presentation will also give you confidence in your subject and yourself.

Ken Blanchard of *One Minute Manager* fame said, "Feedback is the Breakfast of Champions."

In the Air Force, we had another way of saying this: "Train the way you fight, and fight the way you train."

How important is body language to interpersonal communication? According to Professor Albert Mehrabian, Professor Emeritus of Psychology at UCLA, fully 55 percent of communications is attributed to body language, 38 percent to tone of voice, and 7 percent to the actual words used. Think about it. Over half of your communication is your body language. You want your body language to enhance what you are saying and not dilute it. Body language includes eye contact, facial expressions, gestures, posture, and presence.

INCREASE YOUR INFLUENCE WITH YOUR AUDIENCE THROUGH POSITIVE BODY LANGUAGE

credible

Maintain eye contact with a variety of individual people in the audience. Use facial expressions that are appropriate for different parts of your presentation. For example, if you are talking about a particular key part of your subject, squinting your eyes indicates to the audience what you are saying is particularly important.

If possible, don't hold anything in your hand. It cuts down on gestures, which add to getting your point across. Time gestures to parts of your presentation that you want to emphasize. Practice gestures until they seem natural.

Maintain an erect positive posture; don't slump or rock back and forth or forward and backward. It distracts the audience and diminishes your credibility.

Now we come to the elusive part of body language: presence. We all know that action follows thought, but you should also remember that thought can actually follow action. Act as you "own the room" and you will be surprised at how many times this becomes reality.

Why do we dread the question and answer period? We dread this part of our presentation because we don't know exactly what questions will be asked. Earlier, I talked of the best way to determine what level your audience is at is to seek their feedback before the presentation. This is a great way also to find out what questions they may ask during the presentation.

BECOME AN EXPERT AT ANSWERING AUDIENCE QUESTIONS

First, allow the questioner to fully ask their question. You would be surprised to know how many times the speaker actually starts answering the question before the question is fully asked.

Second, make it a practice to repeat the question so that you fully heard the question and understood it. This also gives your mind a mental break to think of a good answer.

It is entirely appropriate for you to ask the questioner a question if you do not have a full understanding of the question. This gives you even more time to prepare an answer.

She prepared meticulously. She tested all her presentation ideas and organization with many others. And then the question and answer period was upon her. It was rough with the audience's knives sharpened. She spent the whole question and answer period answering questions while looking at her feet. What could have prevented this from happening? If she had practiced her question and answer period with others with equally sharpened knives, she would have fared better.

We agreed up front that your job credibility is key in determining your salary, your level of responsibility, and your reputation in your company and, thus, how valuable it would be to you if you could increase your credibility.

We have discussed three ways to increase your credibility: (1) know at what level your audience is at on your subject, (2) ensure your body language enhances your presentation, and (3) become an expert in answering audience questions.

Go forth today and implement these tips, and you too will see your credibility, prestige, and salary increase.

CALL TO ACTION

- Speak at or slightly above the level your audience is on your subject.
- Maintain positive body language when you speak (e.g., maintain eye contact, use meaningful gestures that match your words).
- Eliminate distracting body movement (e.g., slumping, rocking back and forth or side to side, playing with an object in your hands).

"Don't confuse visibility with credibility."

—Harvey MacKay

YOU ARE YOUR PRESENTATION!

*"People don't remember what we think is important.
They remember what they think is important."*
—John Maxwell

DO YOU THINK YOUR slides are your presentation? If you do, you would be making a mistake most speakers make.

Your presentation is your delivery aided by your slides, props, handouts, and other items meant to support your presentation. In other words, you are your message!

As you are presenting, you are constantly fighting the urge of your audience to be distracted from your message. Many things can distract your audience. Annoying speaker mannerisms and utterances, having too much irrelevant information on your slides, and pacing back and forth or side to side while you speak are but a few.

Below are three tips to keep your audience focused on you instead of your slides, the big football game, what they need to get at the grocery store after your presentation, and a thousand and one other things.

ASK QUESTIONS.

 Questions are a great way to engage your audience and bring their attention back to you and your message. Because you are asking the questions, you can focus them on the points you are trying to bring out in your presentation. Just to be clear, these questions you ask are not rhetorical questions not meaning to be answered.

Make it clear that the questions you are asking are meant to be answered by the audience. Ensure the answers from the audience come from a number of people. There will always be one or two people in your audience that have an answer for every question. Resist the urge to acknowledge them on more than one or two questions.

"BLACKOUT" YOUR SLIDES IF YOU ARE NOT REFERRING TO THEM.

 If you leave a slide up after you have exhausted its usefulness, your audience will be distracted reading the slide and will not be paying attention to you. Remember, you are your message. Anything that distracts from you in your presentation distracts from your message. Distractions from your message will diminish your impact on your audience.

STIFLE YOUR DISTRACTING MANNERISMS AND UTTERANCES.

 Any distracting mannerism and utterance by you will distract your audience. I once sat through a briefing when I was in the Air Force. The briefer used "ums" ninety-three

times before I stopped counting. When I was counting those "ums," was I distracted from the briefer's message? Of course I was. Distracting utterances include any sound from your mouth that does not add positively to your message. These utterances also add to the time of your presentation—wasted time.

Some distracting mannerisms include rocking back and forth or side to side, playing with something in your hand, and not timing your gestures properly, just to name a few. The first step to eliminating distracting mannerisms and utterances is to first realize you are doing them. Video recording yourself and evaluating the video go a long way to solving this challenge.

***

If you want to keep the focus of your audience on you and not distractions, ask questions of your audience, "blackout" slides that are not supporting what you are saying at the moment, and eliminate your distracting mannerisms and utterances.

If you do these things, you will be well on your way to focusing your audience on your message!

CALL TO ACTION

- In your presentation, plan to ask specific questions of your audience at the appropriate times.
- "Blackout" your slide if it is not supporting your message at the moment.
- Video record yourself presenting to uncover your distracting mannerisms and utterances in your presentation. Practice your presentation to eliminate or, at least, reduce appreciably these distractions.

"The whole purpose is to enable people to learn. Your mission is not to transmit information but to transform learners."

—Harold D. Stolovitch and Erica J. Keeps

ARE YOUR INTENTIONS KNOWN?

"There is only one way to avoid criticism: do nothing, say nothing, and be nothing."

—Aristotle

IN YOUR LAST PRESENTATION, did your audience know what your intentions were for what they should remember and take action on?

Every presentation you deliver should have a purpose or intention for your audience. Additionally, you should make it explicit what you want them to take action on and in what timeframe they should take action. If you don't, you have the real chance your audience will "stack" your presentation on top the dust heap of all the other presentations they have heard in the last week, month, and year.

Every speaker wants their presentation to be memorable and to have their audience take action on that memory of your presentation. Don't you?

Read on to find out how.

STATE YOUR INTENTIONS UPFRONT

I continuously teach my children that when they drive, they need to ensure they do nothing other drivers would not expect, like changing lanes without a signal. If they do something the other drivers don't expect, the chances for an accident increase dramatically!

Do you deliver your presentations without "signaling" to your audiences upfront the purpose of your presentation? If you do, it is like changing lanes without a signal. The "accident" if you do is to have your audience befuddled as to what you are trying to put across to them.

You need to use a "turn signal" in your presentation upfront to let them know your intentions. If you don't signal your intentions early in your presentation, they will be distracted throughout your presentation and, therefore, wondering what is going to come next and not listening to your message. You should eliminate anything that distracts from your message.

Stating your intentions of your presentation upfront is certainly necessary, but is it sufficient? No, it is not! You must weave your intentions of your presentations throughout your presentation.

RESTATE YOUR INTENTIONS THROUGHOUT YOUR PRESENTATION

So we know stating your intentions upfront is not enough. If you want your audience to remember your intentions, you also need to weave them throughout your presentation.

I teach a recurring course to an audience. In the first half of the class, I heighten the awareness of a problem to the audience. In the second half of the class, I give the audience five steps they can take to lessen the problem. As I go through the five steps, I have them recite all steps we have covered. Any memory expert will tell you repetition is a great way to remember what you are taught.

Repetition is a precursor to a better memory. Covering your intentions throughout your presentation is a great way to make it memorable for your audience. Was there ever a speaker who didn't want that?

So, in your presentation, you have stated your intentions upfront, you have sprinkled your intentions throughout your presentation, and now you are ready to "hit a home run" to solidify your intentions by restating them in your closing.

RE-RESTATE YOUR INTENTIONS AT THE END OF YOUR PRESENTATION

At this point, you may be thinking, "Won't it be enough to repeat my intentions at the beginning and throughout my presentation? Why would I have to repeat my intentions in my closing?"

Well, this is like in baseball with bases loaded and striking out for the last out, leaving three players stranded on base. Ugh!

Wouldn't you rather "hit the ball out of the park" for a "grand slam home run?"

It is the difference, to use a horse racing term, to between "losing by a nose" or "winning by a nose." It has been said, "There are no traffic jams on the extra mile." Go the extra mile, "win by a nose," and deliver a memorable presentation for your audience!

***

To "hit a home run" every time in your presentations, always state your intentions upfront, sprinkle your intentions throughout your presentation, and then "hit a grand slam home run" by solidifying your intentions by restating them in your closing.

Transferring your intentions to your audience in "digestible" amounts in your presentations will make them memorable and, maybe more importantly, will make you memorable to your audience!

CALL TO ACTION

In your next presentation:

- State your intentions upfront in your presentations.
- Sprinkle your intentions throughout your presentation.
- Hit your "grand slam home run" by restating your intentions in your closing.

"Only those who will risk going too far can possibly find out how far one can go."

—T. S. Eliot

PART V: THE FUTURE OF SPEAKING

DOES ANYONE REMEMBER THE term "viewgraph?" Viewgraphs were plastic sheets on which slides were on. Viewgraph machines were used to project viewgraphs on screens. Viewgraphs and viewgraph machines are no longer used because you are now able to build slide decks with programs like Microsoft PowerPoint and project them through computer projectors. Computer projectors are also in real danger of being replaced by huge flatscreen TVs.

I bring up the demise of the traditional viewgraph and viewgraph machine because it makes a point that technology is forever changing every aspect of your life with public speaking not being an exception.

So, Part V is about the march of technology and how it affects your life as a speaker.

Part V covers the following topics:

- Virtual Speaking's Time is Now!
- Speak Virtually to Stay Connected!
- Time to Talk Tech!
- Become Brilliant on the Basics!
- Time to Speak Tech!
- Three Tips for Speaking in the Virtual World
- Three More Tips for Speaking in the Virtual World
- Still Three More Tips for Speaking in the Virtual World

VIRTUAL SPEAKING'S TIME IS NOW!

"A talk is a voyage with purpose, and it must be charted. The man who starts out going nowhere generally gets there."

—Dale Carnegie

IF YOU ARE NOT speaking virtually, you are leaving money on the table. What is virtual speaking? Virtual speaking is speaking to people remotely through your computer using applications such as Zoom, Webex, or Skype.

As a speaker, you might be saying, "But I want to be in front of people speaking live." I think many speakers feel this way, me included. However, if you are ignoring speaking virtually, you are hurting yourself in your pocketbook.

I am going to explore three reasons why you should supplement your live speaking with speaking virtually.

YOU CAN REACH MANY MORE PEOPLE

Believe it or not, 3.5 billion of the 7.5 billion people in the world have Internet service. That's 3.5 billion people it is possible to reach with your virtual speaking. If you only reach 0.1 percent of these people, that is 3.5 million people. If you only reach 0.01 percent of these people, that is 350,000 people. If you only reach 0.001 percent, that is still 35,000 people. By leveraging the power of the Internet, you can service an enormous amount of people.

Now, of course, all the people you reach will not become customers. Let's say you reach 0.01 percent of the people on the Internet and only one percent are buying customers. That would mean you have 3,500 people who are buying customers, and a large majority of these customers are probably repeat customers. What business wouldn't like that customer base?

Not only does virtual speaking reach many more people than live speaking, it reduces your costs tremendously.

REDUCES COSTS

Because your virtual learning experience happens in the comfort of your office or home, there are no transportation, hotel, or time costs. Time costs are the money you spend to travel to the airport near your speaking venue, travel from the airport to your hotel and check into your hotel, and setting up your laptop computer in your hotel room. When you speak remotely, these costs are saved and can be used for other important things like generating leads, satisfying your customers, or answering critical e-mail messages.

If you are an employer or an entrepreneur, virtual meetings create efficiency because your team could be dispersed around the country and/or around the world. In fact, you may never meet your employees and/or consultants face-to-face.

Now, don't get me wrong. There are real advantages to meeting in person. However, in business, there is a balancing act that is performed by every business owner every day in determining the return on investment of bringing people together in one place or meeting virtually. Only the business owner can decide which is more advantageous for his or her business. However, technology has advanced to the point where it is very easy for anyone to set up a virtual meeting and meet virtually.

So, virtual speaking reaches many more people than live speaking, and it reduces your costs tremendously. But did you know that it can provide an additional stream of income when you are sleeping?

AN ADDITIONAL MULTIPLE STREAM OF INCOME

We all have twenty-four hours in a day, seven days a week, 365 days a year. If you only get paid by your customers when you are speaking live, there will be an upper limit on your business's earnings. Any service you provide where you are trading your time for being paid by your customers limits the possible income from live speaking.

Virtual speaking is an additional stream of income for your business. We have already talked about the vastly greater number of people you can reach and the costs you can save by speaking virtually. In addition to selling your live virtual speaking, you can sell the recording of this speaking, whether it be a webinar, a keynote address delivered virtually, one-on-one coaching, or many other methods of delivering your services.

The best part of speaking virtually is through the technology of the mechanism you use. You can record your virtual speaking and either sell the whole video or divide the video into parts and sell them separately. Here is where the selling while you are sleeping comes in. Post these videos in your web site store so people around the world can benefit and, yes, pay for the privilege of watching you in action.

***

In this chapter, I have touched on but three advantages of speaking virtually. There are many more. Below are links to three articles that talk about the advantages and disadvantages of speaking virtually. They're a good read.

- Advantages and Downside of Virtual Meeting Services (https://www.business2community.com/cloud-computing/advantages-and-downside-of-virtual-meeting-services-0398623)
- The Eight Benefits of Virtual Meetings (https://www.eztalks.com/video-meeting/benefits-of-virtual-meetings.html)
- What Are the Benefits of Virtual Meetings? (https://www.pgi.com/resources/articles/biggest-benefits-virtual-meetings/)

Virtual speaking reaches many more people than live speaking, reduces your costs tremendously, and provides an additional stream of income.

Are you interested in earning more income? I am!

CALL TO ACTION

- Read books and articles on the Internet on how to develop, deliver, and market webinars and then put what you learn into action.
- Total the transportation, hotel, time costs, and any other costs from having to travel to your last speaking venue to see how much money you would be saving if you spoke virtually.
- Develop estimates of how much additional income you will make from selling recordings of your webinars.

"Many attempts to communicate are nullified by saying too much."

—Robert Greenleaf

SPEAK VIRTUALLY TO STAY CONNECTED!

"Only the prepared speaker deserves to be confident."
—Dale Carnegie

AS LONG AS HUMANS continue to speak, there will be demand for someone to speak live to an audience. This is not going away. However, with virtual tool technologies now available to anyone with a computer and Internet connection, the options for speakers have increased dramatically.

Any speaker who is not speaking virtually is "leaving money on the table." This chapter will explore virtual tool features, virtual tool considerations, and a sampling (non-inclusive) of virtual tools.

Notice that I don't say "virtual learning tool," "virtual meeting tool," or "virtual presentation tool," because virtual tools can be used for all of these purposes and much more. The catchall phrase will be "virtual session tool."

VIRTUAL TOOL FEATURES

Let me, upfront, say that here we are not talking about virtual reality. We are talking about computer tools you can use on your computer that connect you to one or more people by audio and video.

Below are seven key Virtual Session Tool features:

- <u>Breakout Rooms</u> – The virtual session host's ability to randomly or selectively choose specific people and send them to a virtual breakout space where they can collaborate by video and audio privately. Usually, there is a feature available to participants to leave the breakout room and return to the main room of the virtual session.
- <u>Background Change</u> – The ability of any virtual session participant to change the background of their video feed to a standard background or one of their choosing.
- <u>Chat Room</u> – Similar to various instant messenger systems, this is a box on your screen where you can text a message to everyone or any one person privately in the virtual session.
- <u>Host-Only Capabilities (non-inclusive)</u>
    - Mute everyone in the session.
    - Send random or host pre-assigned participants to breakout rooms.
    - Send everyone a message in each breakout room.
    - Bring participants in breakout rooms back into the main room.

- <u>Mute Audio / turn off camera</u> – All virtual session participants have the ability to mute their audio and turn their video on and off.
- <u>Screen Sharing</u> – The ability for the meeting host or any participant to share his/her screen including videos during a live virtual session.
- <u>Speaker/Gallery Views</u> – Every participant has the ability to switch video feeds between the speaker (Speaker View) and all video feeds of everyone in the virtual session (Gallery View).

Once you understand virtual session tool features, the next step is learn what considerations are important when deciding which virtual session tool is right for you.

VIRTUAL TOOL CONSIDERATIONS

It is important to know there are three distinct roles in each virtual session: speaker, moderator, and participant.

- <u>Speaker</u> – The person who is the subject matter expert, gives the presentation and takes questions. They may, on occasion respond to individual chat questions and comments. I say occasionally because the job of reading every individual question and comment in the chat is better left up to the host.

- The reason for this is that if the speaker reads every individual question and comment in the chat, it seriously affects the flow of the presentation. It is the host's job to group questions and comments and then present them orally to the speaker so he or she can address them. A separate audio feed like a phone call between host and presenter is recommended.
- Speakers that are unfamiliar with virtual sessions usually think they can present and also manage the virtual session. This is a mistake. If the speaker tries to do both, both will suffer. ***ALWAYS HAVE A HOST IN ANY LIVE VIRTUAL SESSION***. You will be very glad you did.
- <u>Host</u> – Introduces the participants to the virtual meeting, introduces the speaker, and reads the individual questions and comments in the chat to group them and then present them to the speaker so he or she can address them.
  - The host also has the power to mute or unmute any participant. He or she also looks for signals from the participants such as raised hands, applause, etc.
  - As I mentioned above, the host controls the virtual session, including assigning and putting participants in breakout rooms.
  - The moderator also thanks the speaker and closes the virtual session.
- <u>Participant</u> – Person attending the virtual session. Participants have duties in the session also. Participants can mute or unmute their audio and video. They can add questions or comments to the chat. They can also return to the main room from a breakout room. They can give signals such as a raised hand, thumbs up, and applause in response to the speaker.

When you are selecting a specific virtual session tool, consider the following:

- <u>Virtual Tool Features</u> – Decide what features you want available to the speaker, moderator, and participant. Just like you would have a list of desired features when buying a car, the same goes for when you buy a virtual session tool.
- <u>Level of Service</u> – Most virtual session tools have two or three levels of service depending on your individual needs. The most basic services usually limit the number of people in a particular session and the number of minutes you can meet. Like the "momma bear's porridge" being "just right," you need to match the service to ensure they are "just right" in satisfying your present and future requirements.
- <u>Ease of Use</u> – Ease of use applies to the speaker, moderator, and participant. In this world of instant apps and lightning speed Internet, if a participant has a hard time getting into the virtual session or using the tool while in the session, he or she will never come back for the next seminar. If the host cannot control the session easily, it will be very choppy and uncomfortable for the speaker and participant and the moderator.
- <u>Cost</u> – Cost will be determined by what features you need, which will determine the level of service you need and, therefore, the cost of the tool/level of service you purchase. These two plus ease of use have to be analyzed to see if the contemplated cost is a good return on investment.

Once you understand virtual session tool features and you have decided what considerations are important when deciding which tool is right for you, the final step is to become familiar with available tools, decide which tool is the most appropriate for you, purchase it, and use it.

VIRTUAL TOOLS – A SAMPLING

Below are a sampling of virtual session tools I have used. This list does not constitute my endorsement nor is it a complete list of available virtual session tools.

- GoToWebinar – Focused more on one-way presentations from the meeting speaker to his/her audience and has participation features limited to audio only with no video. In other words, as a participant, you will see the video of the speaker but will not be able to control it. (www. gotomeeting.com)
- GoToMeeting – Web-hosted service. It is an online meeting, desktop sharing, and video conferencing software package that enables the user to meet with other computer users, customers, clients, or colleagues via the Internet in real time.
    - GoToMeeting contains more features to allow interactive participation in the meeting, via video conferencing and document and desktop sharing than GoToWebinar. (www.gotomeeting.com)
- Skype – Telecommunications application that specializes in providing video chat and voice calls between computers, tablets, mobile devices, the Xbox One console, and smartwatches over the Internet. Skype also provides instant messaging services. Users may transmit text, video, audio and images. (www.skype.com)

- <u>Webex</u> – Web-based video collaboration service with the following non-inclusive features: screen sharing, audio/video mute/unmute, breakout rooms, chat, speaker/gallery views. (www.webex.com)
- <u>Zoom</u> – Web-based video collaboration service with the following non-inclusive features: screen sharing, audio/video mute/unmute, breakout rooms, chat, speaker/gallery views. (www.zoom.com)

So, what have you learned? You have learned the most used virtual session tool features, you have decided what considerations are important when deciding which tool is right for you, and you have become familiar with available tools. You have also learned it is important to decide which tool is the most appropriate for you. Purchase it and use it.

Buy and use a virtual session tool. Jump in. The water's fine!

CALL TO ACTION

- Decide what virtual session tool features are most important to you.
- Test out virtual session tools for the thirty-day free trials.
- Decide what virtual session tool is right for you, purchase it, and use it.

"He who wants to persuade should put his trust not in the right argument, but in the right word. The power of sound has always been greater than the power of sense."

—Joseph Conrad

TIME TO TALK TECH!

"Eloquence is the power to translate a truth into language perfectly intelligible to the person to whom you speak."

—Ralph Waldo Emerson

HAVE YOU GIVEN THE same presentation twenty times and are looking for a way to "spice up" your presentation? Look no further than at technology that is available to you right now!

Breathe new life into your presentations by polling your audience, using smart glasses, and embedding videos in your slides.

POLLING YOUR AUDIENCE

 As a speaker, you should always try to engage with your audience in various ways. You ask them questions. You have them ask questions of you. You pass around a "show and tell" object

relevant to your topic. Have you ever thought of polling your audience during your presentation?

What is the one thing you see in everybody's hands nowadays? Right! They have their smartphone in their hands. Why not poll your audience through their smartphones during your presentation? There are services available to you right now to allow you to do this. Here is how it works.

You set up a set of questions online on one of the polling services. Then, during your presentation, you ask your audience to go to a certain website to answer your questions. The polling service instantly calculates statistics from your audience's answers they input through their own smartphone. Then you display the answers on the screen in real time and draw conclusions, on the spot, from your audience's answers to the poll questions. What could be easier? Google "polling your audience" to discover the latest polling services.

Polling is great, but have you ever had the urge to look back at your slides and away from your audience?

SMART GLASSES

We have all had the urge when we are presenting to look behind us at our slides to determine if we are on the correct slide, to remember a point from the slide, or just as a matter of habit. What if I said you could still see your slides without ever turning around again? Enter smart glasses.

What if there could be a device that could display your presentations so you would be able to see them as you are facing your audience? This technology is currently commercially available. Military pilots have been using this technology (heads-up display) for decades.

Smart glasses project your slides and anything else on the master computer screen on a set of glasses you can wear during your presentation. Google "smart glasses" to discover the latest smart glasses.

Polling is a crowd pleaser and smart glasses will give you the feeling of presenting on the command deck of the Starship *Enterprise*, but what can you do to keep your audience from getting bored? Enter embedded videos in your presentation.

EMBEDDED VIDEOS IN YOUR PRESENTATION

Your audience will get bored easily if you don't vary your presentation method (e.g., briefing a slide, audience exercises, polling using your audience members, etc.).

One of the great ways to vary your presentation method is to show short videos relevant to your topic. Emphasis on the word "short"—one to two minutes. Remember the videos must support your presentation and not take it over. Longer videos have a tendency to do this.

I gave a presentation a few weeks ago and embedded some YouTube videos. They were a hit! Ninety-nine percent of the time, you would not want to use the complete YouTube video. You just want to use a part of the video. No problem. There is a way to start and end YouTube videos for whatever part you want. Just Google "embedding YouTube videos in a PowerPoint" to find out how to do this. It's easy. Trust me.

***

So, today, you learned about three ways to use technology to enhance your presentations: polling your audience, using smart glasses to see your presentation while you are still facing your audience, and embedding videos in your presentation.

Try all three of these and you may feel like Captain Kirk giving orders on the command deck of the Starship *Enterprise*!

CALL TO ACTION

- Use polling in your next presentation.
- Investigate the state-of-the-art smart glasses. Consider using them in your next presentation.
- Use at least one relevant video clip in your next presentation.

"If you can't state your position in eight words, you don't have a position."

—Seth Godin

BECOME BRILLIANT ON THE BASICS!

"The best way to predict the future is to create it."

—Brian Tracy

THE VAST MAJORITY OF us are enamored with technology. Virtual meetings, polling your audience, and holographic figures on the stage are but a few of the technological innovations here today, and more are coming tomorrow, next month, and next year.

When I say the "future of public speaking," I am sure these technology marvels first come to mind. While these technological inventions are great for you in your presentations, technology is not your message. You are your message!

It is important to remember that technology is only useful if it supports your message. A quick way to distract your audience and maybe make them mad at you is to use technology for technology's sake and not support your message.

Vince Lombardi, the legendary coach of the Green Bay Packers football team, on taking over as head coach of the

Packers, said, "I am not going to change anything. We will use the same players, the same plays, and the same training system. But we will concentrate on becoming **_brilliant on the basics_**."

So, in this chapter, I will give you some tips on being **_brilliant on the basics_** of public speaking. This has always been and always will be the foundation of any great presentation. It has been the past, present, and will be the future of great public speaking.

All presentation preparation must start with a thorough analysis of your audience. Without this, you are out in a rowboat in a lake with no paddle and no rudder. You are always the "paddle" and your audience is always the "rudder" for any presentation you prepare and deliver.

***

So what does your audience want? Your audience wants (1) your presentation in actuality as it is advertised, (2) information they can immediately use, and (3) your presentation to be entertaining and informative.

YOUR AUDIENCE WANTS YOUR PRESENTATION TO BE AS ADVERTISED

Imagine an action movie being advertised as action packed while the actual movie has 90 percent more dialogue than action. False advertising!

Imagine you buy that just released mystery bestseller advertised as a mystery reader's mystery and you discover clues that are not veiled, halfway through the book you pretty much know "whodunit," and at the end of the book, the author lets the killer get away with it. False advertising!

Imagine you buy a lawn weed trimmer advertised with a battery that has over an hour of operational life, and after twenty minutes, the weed trimmer goes dead. Boy, did you get rooked! False advertising.

Your job as a speaker is to ensure your audience gets everything in your presentation you advertise. I will go further. You should give your audience more than they paid for. This could take several forms of extras.

Maybe you will give everyone in your audience a free half hour of telephone consultation time with you. It could be a free PDF report of ten of your most popular articles in one package. It could even be a deep discount on one of your programs. Just give them more than they paid for. It will keep them coming back.

This is a great way to get repeat customers. It takes seven times the effort and time to create a new customer. Repeat customers are like "gold" and at a fraction of the effort to create a new customer.

Making your presentation more than advertised is a great way to have them come back for more. Remember, repeat customers are like "gold."

Outstanding Speaker Secret #1: Give your audience more in your presentation than advertised.

Have you ever gone to a presentation and come out and said, "That was a great presentation, but what do I do with this information?" Your audiences have the same question. If you don't show your audience how they can immediately use the information in your presentation to better their personal or professional lives, you would have missed a golden opportunity to create repeat customers.

YOUR AUDIENCE WANTS INFORMATION THEY CAN IMMEDIATELY USE

You are in the audience listening to the speaker's presentation. What is the first question in your mind? What's in it for me (WIIFM)? The great speaker will answer this question completely and has the answer to your next question: "How can I use the speaker's information right now?"

You need to be ready to answer both of these questions well before you start your presentation. Here is the thing. You will probably never be asked these questions explicitly. However, you need to give the answers somewhere in your presentation.

The only way to answer these questions is to analyze your audience. What is your audience's demographic makeup? What expertise do they have on your topic? What is their opinion of your topic? This is not an inclusive list of questions. There are many more questions, but you get the idea.

It is common sense that if you want to give your audience information they can immediately use, you have to have a deep understanding of what your audience expects and needs from your presentation.

The best speakers include a part at the end of their presentations for a Call to Action to the audience. Think of these actions the way you think of SMART goals: specific, measurable, attainable, relevant, and time-based.

If you describe these actions this way, you will completely answer your audience's questions, "What's in it for me?" and "How can I use this information right now?"

Outstanding Speaker Secret #2: Charge your audience to complete SMART actions they can do right now.

So you now know your presentation should exceed its advertisement and how you need to give your audience SMART actions to accomplish after the presentation.

As the third piece of advice in this trifecta of giving the audience what they want, you need to be entertaining. You need to grab your audience's attention at the beginning of your presentation and don't let go until your presentation is done. One way to do this is to be entertaining. When your audience is having a good time, their minds will be open to your ideas and actions for them.

YOUR AUDIENCE WANTS TO BE ENTERTAINED

 Why do you go to see a movie? Why do you attend your favorite football team's game? Why do you read your favorite author's books? Of course, because you want to be entertained. The good feelings you feel during and after being entertained open your mind to new things. It is the same thing with being entertaining when you speak before your audience.

Now, entertaining could take many forms. It could be something you say that is quite humorous to your audience. You could tell a poignant story that tugs at your audience's emotions. You could give them a tip that will greatly improve their lives. It could be many things.

Let's first talk about humor. When I say humor, I do not mean comedy. Humor is not about telling jokes, acting goofy, or telling a riddle. What is humor? Humor is leading your audience down a specific track and then taking them down a completely different track.

It is important your humor follow these three rules: (1) it cannot be off-color, (2) it must be relevant to your topic, and (3) it can never be at the expense of someone else. The reason to follow these three rules is if you don't, you will offend someone in the audience. Throughout your whole speaking career, avoid offending your audiences like the plague.

Some of the best humor I have seen in other speakers, and I have used myself, is self-deprecating humor. This type of humor is okay in small doses. Don't use this type of humor more than two or three times in your presentation. The reason for this is two-fold: using self-deprecating humor more than three times will start to "chip away" at your credibility, and after two or three times, self-deprecating humor becomes tiresome to your audience.

Poignant stories with a powerful message are the best way to get your audience to remember your presentation. Stories of redemption, overcoming suffering, and learning a valuable lesson are very powerful tools in your speaking "quiver."

Interweaving stories in your presentations accomplishes three things for you: (1) stories grab the attention of your audience, (2) stories give your audience "hooks" so they can remember your main points, and (3) stories tap the emotions of your audience.

Stories are older than the printing press, the ancient Romans and Greeks, and recorded history. In fact, the first recording of history was through the stories passed from generation to generation. There is a reason for stories to still be around. Everybody loves a good story!

Outstanding Speaker Secret #3: Entertain your audience while also teaching them and they will be as attentive to your presentation as any audience could be.

***

So what have you learned about your audience from this chapter? You have learned (1) the benefits of delivering more in your presentation than advertised, (2) to give your audience information they can immediately use, and (3) to entertain your audience as you are teaching them.

Technology will advance and, no doubt, affect the speaking arena, but the foundation of any great presentation in the past, the present, and in the future is to be ***brilliant on the basics***. The basics were there in the past, are there today, and will be there in the future!

CALL TO ACTION

- Deliver more than your presentation is advertised.
- Charge your audience to complete SMART (specific, measurable, attainable, relevant, time-based) actions they can do right now.
- Entertain your audience while also teaching them.

"Our future will be shaped by the assumptions we make about who we are and what we can be."

—Rosabeth Moss Kanter

TIME TO SPEAK TECH!

"Your work is going to fill a large part of your life, and the only way to be truly satisfied is to do what you believe is great work. And the only way to do great work is to love what you do. If you haven't found it yet, keep looking. Don't settle. As with all matters of the heart, you'll know when you find it."

—Steve Jobs

ARE THERE DIFFERENCES BETWEEN a technical and non-technical presentation?

I would say this. There are certain areas in technical presentations that will cause you particular problems. Because of the technical nature of your subject, these problems have a tendency to be magnified in technical presentations.

Read on to find out what they are!

DO YOU KNOW WHAT YOUR AUDIENCE KNOWS ABOUT YOUR TECHNICAL TOPIC?

 You are giving a briefing on Quantum Computing. Well before your presentation, can you answer the following questions?

- What is my audience's expertise concerning Quantum Computing?
- What does my audience want to know about Quantum Computing?
- What does my audience need to know about Quantum Computing?

If you cannot answer these questions well before your presentation, there is almost a 100 percent chance that you will miss an opportunity to present information your audience will find useful.

Although failing to analyze the audience is a malady suffered by both technical and non-technical speakers, I think this is a "steeper climb" to accomplish this for your technical presentations. Read below to find out why.

Technical subjects have many more details associated with them than do more general topics such as the next election, child rearing, and yoga. Also, the percentage of the general population who knows anything about your technical topic is much smaller than the percentage of the general population who knows anything about a general topic like the next election, child rearing, and yoga.

What does this mean? It means there is a lower and maybe much lower chance that anyone in your audience has knowledge of your topic as compared with a general topic.

Without knowledge of what your audience knows about your technical topic, you are "in the middle of a large lake without a paddle or rudder." Knowledge of your audience is the "paddle" and "rudder" for your presentation. Knowledge of your audience provides the necessary foundation of a great and useful presentation.

Too many speakers ask the question, "What do I want to talk about in my presentation?" instead of "What does my audience want to hear and what do they need to learn from my presentation?"

So, the first step is to look to your audience to find the answers to the three questions above.

The next point centers around presentation detail. Engineers and scientists love detail. That is why they pursued a degree in engineering or science. Too much detail is almost always detrimental in your technical presentations.

WHEN IN DOUBT, TAKE IT OUT!

 This love for detail actually blinds us engineers and scientists to the amount of material to put on our slides and the detail to put into our speaking. As in other professions, engineers and scientists are proud of their work and rightfully so. They, like the rest of speakers, want to tell others what they are working on. Remember, though, your presentation is for your audience, not you!

However, the propensity to tell our audiences all there is to know about our subject is strong and needs to be overcome if you are truly going to give your audience what they want and what they need from your presentation.

The best rule of thumb is, "When in doubt, take it out." As mentioned above, the "paddle" and "rudder" to prepare your presentation is your audience.

While developing your presentation, constantly ask yourself the question, "Does my audience need this information to fulfill the purpose of my presentation?" And you know by now the purpose of your presentation is always determined by what your audience wants and needs from your presentation.

So you know the first step in developing a presentation is to answer the three questions in the first section. You also know whenever you are in doubt of adding specific information, the wise thing is to take it out. A corollary of this is when in doubt, if you can reduce your doubt sufficiently, leave the information in your presentation.

However, one of the hardest challenges to overcome for all speakers, not only technical ones, is the propensity of your audience's attention to wander to other things and not stay totally focused on your topic. Unnecessary detail in your slides and what you say unrelated or, at best, tangentially related to your presentation purpose has a tendency to distract your audience.

"SEPARATE THE WHEAT FROM THE CHAFF"

There is an old farming expression that says, "Separate the wheat from the chaff." If you have ever farmed, you know what I am talking about.

"Wheat" is good. "Chaff" is bad. The "wheat" in your presentation is the information you need your audience to take away from your presentation. The "chaff" in your presentation is the information your audience does not need to take away. The "chaff" is often somewhat related information that your audience may find interesting but does not need to take away from your presentation. Your job is to keep the "wheat" and discard the "chaff."

The "chaff" in your presentation could be in your slides, videos, exercises, and even in the words you speak.

As a writer, I know that reuse of relevant content saves time. Newsletters turn into blogs, which turn into social media posts, which turn into books, etc. It is smart to do this. It saves a lot of time. It is very efficient and, if done correctly, is very effective for your target audience.

However, too many times engineers and scientists don't perform a quality check on content to ensure their audiences really need to know everything on a slide or in what they say. Yes, I mean look at every slide, video, and what you are going to say to see if it passes the "Does my audience need to know this?" test.

It takes some time to do this, but is it better to have some short-term pain for long-term gain or the other way around? Short-term gain for long-term pain is, to be sure, faster, but it will never provide the long-term gain you are looking for and produce a great presentation.

This being said, as you spend years in certain subject areas, you will build up quite a lot of slides and videos on your topic. A judicious selection of these slides/videos for a particular presentation is okay if you want to "hit singles and doubles (baseball analogy)." However, if you want to "hit a home run" with all your presentations, review the selection of the previous slides you developed and planned to use for particular relevance to your current audience.

If there are five items of information on the slide and your current topic only requires three of these five items, take out the two not needed before you present to your current audience. You won't "hit a home run" all the time, but your chances go up dramatically of "hitting one."

***

So what have you learned today?

- You learned the first step in developing a presentation is to answer the three questions:
  - What is my audience's expertise concerning my technical topic?
  - What does my audience want to know about my technical topic?
  - What does my audience need to know about my technical topic?
- You also learned a good rule of thumb is whenever you are in doubt of adding specific information, the wise thing is to take it out. A corollary of this is when in doubt, if you can reduce your doubt sufficiently, leave the information in your presentation.
- Finally, you learned unnecessary detail in your slides and what you say unrelated or, at best, tangentially related to your presentation purpose has a tendency to distract your audience. "Separate your wheat from your chaff."

So heed these the next time you prepare and deliver a technical presentation.

You want to "hit a home run," don't you?

CALL TO ACTION

- Before you prepare your next presentation, find out:
  - What is my audience's expertise concerning my technical topic?
  - What does my audience want to know about my technical topic?
  - What does my audience need to know about my technical topic?
- While you are preparing your next presentation, if you have any doubt about whether you should use a particular item of information, don't use it.

- Also, while you are preparing your next presentation, "separate the wheat from the chaff." Only use information, your audience absolutely needs to use.

"A bad attitude is like a flat tire. You can't go anywhere till you change it."

—Earl Nightingale

THREE TIPS FOR SPEAKING IN THE VIRTUAL WORLD

"Developing strong public speaking skills may be the difference between enjoying the high level of success you've envisioned or looking back on your career with regret."

—Peter George

YOU'VE BEEN SPEAKING IN person for quite some time and doing well. How hard can it be to transfer your speaking to the virtual world? Think again. It can be very hard. The virtual world puts a number of restrictions on your speaking.

This chapter presents three tips for presenting in the virtual world. Connecting with the audience, displaying meaningful gestures, and varying your voice's pitch and pace are three great ways to come close to recreating your in-person delivery in the virtual world.

It is challenging enough speaking in person. However, when your speaking is in the virtual world, it behooves you to think of ways to stand out in the virtual event.

AUDIENCE CONNECTION

 Your ability to connect with your audience is critical to the success of your presentation. Now, connecting with the audience is a tall order when you are presenting in-person. It becomes even harder when you present virtually. Below are some tips that will help you establish and maintain a connection with your audience.

When you are one screen amongst ten or twenty-five or fifty screens, it is easy for someone to tune you out.

You have heard that people remember things at the beginning and end of a presentation. A dramatic opening, although necessary in an in-person presentation, is critical during a virtual presentation. Remember, it is easy for people in a virtual presentation to actually be working on something else on their computers while you are speaking. This is what you are trying to prevent. In my virtual coaching, I actually ask people to resist the urge to do other work.

Four ways you might use to present a dramatic opening are a poignant quote, a startling statistic, a heartwarming story, or a question that makes them think. You need to grab the audience's attention at the start of your presentation and not let go even after your presentation has ended.

Allow and respond to/answer comments and questions in the chat box. Answer them as best you can during your presentation. Better yet, have a host summarize the questions/comments in the chat for you so you can concentrate on your presentation while answering or responding to a group's questions and comments.

GESTURES

I think you would agree gestures add greatly to getting your point across to your audience. The next time you are logged into a virtual event, notice how little of your body is shown. This affects your gestures greatly. For someone who normally gestures at his or her waist level, others on the virtual event will not even see your gestures.

There are two ways to ensure your gestures are seen by everyone.

The first way to ensure your gestures are seen by everyone is to simply raise your gestures to your chest or above level. It is easy to check to see whether your gestures are visible because you can see yourself on your screen.

The second method to ensure your gestures are seen by everyone is to back up from your computer until your body from at least your waist up is shown. This method has other advantages. The more of your body that can be shown on the screen, the more you can use body language besides gestures. This is my preferred method of ensuring my gestures are seen and, therefore, support my presentation appropriately.

Earl Nightingale, one of my mentors, says, "The only obligation of a speaker is to be interesting." Connecting with your audience and displaying meaningful gestures are two great ways you can be a more interesting speaker. A third way is to vary the pitch of your voice at appropriate times in your presentation.

VOCAL VARIETY

I am sure you have heard a speaker with a monotone. There is no emphasis on anything they are saying. Speaking in a monotone is boring to an audience. One of the main reasons for speaking in a monotone is the speaker is speaking too fast. In his or her effort to get through all the material they have planned, there is no time to vary the pitch of his or her voice. The solution is to leave in the critical material and take out the not so critical material.

It is vitally important when you speak virtually to vary the pitch and pace of your voice. You are restricted when you speak virtually. One of the ways to combat these restrictions is to vary your voice pitch and pace even more than would be needed if you were speaking at an in-person event.

At a virtual event, you need to stand out more. You are not on a stage with all the advantages that gives you as a speaker—you stand out from the audience, they are all looking at you instead of other people on other screens, you can read the audience much better than in the virtual world, to name just a few.

***

Discussion and executing plans of how we can more closely create the in-person speaking experience with the virtual speaking experience is needed now more than ever.

Connecting with the audience, displaying meaningful gestures, and varying your voice's pitch and pace are three great ways to enhance your virtual speaking.

It is challenging enough speaking in person. However, when your speaking is in the virtual world, it behooves you to think of ways to stand out from the other videos in the virtual event.

This virtual world was thrust upon us speakers. The speakers that adjust to it, embrace it, and create new virtual ways to get their messages across to their audiences will still thrive. Those speakers who don't won't.

Which speaker do you want to be?

CALL TO ACTION

- Use poignant quote, a startling statistic, a heartwarming story, or a question in the opening and closing of your next virtual presentation.
- Ensure your gestures are seen in your next virtual presentation.
- Vary your voice's pitch and pace to keep your audiences on the edge of their seats during your next virtual presentation.

"The ability to simplify means to eliminate the unnecessary so that the necessary may speak."

—Hans Hoffman

THREE MORE TIPS FOR SPEAKING IN THE VIRTUAL WORLD

"Best way to conquer stage fright is to know what you are talking about."

—Michael Mescon

IN THE PREVIOUS CHAPTER, I gave you three tips for speaking in the virtual world.

This week, I give your three more tips: Increase your distance from the camera, properly position your lighting, and get more personal with your audience.

DISTANCE FROM YOUR CAMERA

When you are delivering an in-person presentation, your audience sees all of you: your face, your arms, your legs, etc. You use your body language to communicate.

I have mentioned previously the fact that studies have shown your body language and tone of voice are the vast majority of your communication.

However, now you are presenting in this virtual world, and the limits on what the audience can see of you are the dimensions your little video box.

When you are attending a virtual meeting, there are people at different distances from their cameras. For some, all you can see is their face. For others, they are far away from the camera. You might not be able to make out their facial expressions.

So how do you maximize your communication within your little video box?

If you are sitting for your presentation, increase your distance to the camera enough so the audience can see you from your waist up. Do this because your gestures and your upper body language can then be seen. How many speakers have you listened to and observed virtually whose gestures and upper body language are hidden? Don't negate your body language by being too close to your camera.

Even better than sitting for your presentation is to stand further away from your camera so the audience can see you from your knees up. By virtue of standing, your body language will be more pronounced.

There is one caution on standing for your presentation. Be sure to know the left and right boundaries of your camera. Put white tape on the floor on the left and right to signify the left and right camera boundaries and where you should not go.

So distance from the camera contributes mightily to your communication to the audience.

Although increasing your distance to the camera will help with your body language, it won't solve your lighting challenge.

LIGHTING

I hold a number of presentation and interview skills courses in the virtual world. In every class, I see lighting problems on the students' screens. Sometimes, someone looks like a shadow. You would think they are in the witness protection program.

A good rule of thumb is your lighting should be facing you and not behind you. If it is behind you, you will look like a shadow. People will not be able to discern your facial expressions. Quite often, I see people on the screen with a window in the background. Avoid this if possible.

Even if the lighting is in front of you, there is always the chance it will cast shadows.

An instructor in one of the virtual courses I took said the best lighting is to have two lights of the same lighting magnitude shining at you on angles toward you away from the center of your face. This eliminates shadows.

So you have learned the importance of maintaining some distance from your camera and the proper placement of lighting. The third and last tip this week is to get more personal with your audience.

GET MORE PERSONAL

Now what do I mean by get more personal?

When you are delivering an in-person presentation, it is important to let the audience know who you are. Your audience will then connect with you more.

In the virtual world, however, the audience only sees you in that little video box. Because there is additional distancing from your audience in the virtual world (you are literally not in your audience's presence), it is especially hard to establish and maintain a connection with your audience.

One way to establish a connection with your audience is to allow your audience to know a little bit more of your personal life than you would normally tell them in an in-person presentation.

The more you open up about your personal life, the more commonality your audience will find with you and, therefore, connect with you more.

Now, let me clarify. I am not asking you to open your whole life; just a little more than you would if you were presenting in person.

For instance, in an in-person delivery, you might mention you are married and have four kids. In a virtual delivery, you might want to name your kids and tell a little about their backgrounds (e.g., high school, college, sports, etc.). That is the extent I am talking about. I am not talking about mentioning how your brother-in-law is serving time, describing your knee operation or discussing your experience in the third grade.

A funny thing happens when you open up a little more to your audience. Audience members start comparing their lives and kids to your life and kids. They will find commonalities. Commonalities brings people closer. It establishes you as a person to whom your audience should be listening. What speaker does not want that?

So next time you are speaking virtually, try a little more openness with your life. The audience connection benefits will be worth it!

***

What have you learned in this chapter? You have learned how increasing your distance from your camera exposes your body language and, therefore, increases your communication. You learned lighting should be in front of you and not behind you. Finally, you learned letting your audience know a bit more about your personal life than you would volunteer in an in-person presentation actually draws the audience more toward you.

As you navigate this virtual world of speaking, you will notice similarities and differences between this world and the in-person world. Keep doing what you would do in the in-person world. Realize the differences between in-person and virtual presentations. Make plans to adjust and take advantage of the differences.

There may be a resistance from you to pursue virtual speaking.

When automobiles first came on the scene in the early twentieth century, horse-drawn buggy manufacturers still thought they were in the horse-drawn buggy manufacturing business. They were wrong! They were in the transportation business. If another transportation method came along that was cheaper, cleaner, and more economical, they would be out of business. The rest is history!

How many horse-drawn buggies are sold each year in this country? How many automobiles are sold in this country every year?

Thinking speaking can only be done in-person is old world thinking and dangerous if you earn your living from speaking. Thinking speaking can be done in both the in-person and virtual worlds is new world thinking.

Make no mistake. We are now in a new hybrid speaking world!

Would you rather sell horse-drawn buggies or automobiles? You decide!

CALL TO ACTION

In your next virtual presentation:

- Increase your distance from your camera to increase your communication.
- See the light by ensuring your lighting is in front of you and not in back of you.
- Provide a bit more about your personal life than you would in an in-person presentation to establish a stronger connection with your audience in the virtual world.

"Ninety percent of how well the talk will go is determined before the speaker steps on the platform."

—Somers White

STILL THREE MORE TIPS FOR SPEAKING IN THE VIRTUAL WORLD

"There are good leaders who actively guide and bad leaders who actively misguide. Hence, leadership is about persuasion, presentation and people skills."
—Shiv Kera

IN THE LAST TWO chapters, I have given you six tips for speaking in the virtual world.

In this chapter, I give you three final tips for speaking in the virtual world: use speaker view, ensure your background matches your message, and use high-speed Internet.

USE SPEAKER VIEW

 You've just started a class on Zoom that has thirty people in it. Your students all appear on your screen in tiny video boxes. If someone asks

you a question or has a comment, how do you determine who it is? The answer is speaker view.

You have two choices in Zoom as to how to display your audience. Gallery view displays everyone in your audience at the same time. This makes it very hard to determine who is currently speaking.

However, speaker view allows the person who is currently speaking to appear very large on your screen. This way, it is very easy to determine who is currently speaking. In speaker view, you can still see the others in their little video boxes, but you might have to scroll left or right or from top or bottom to get to a particular person.

We know that engaging your audience in a virtual world is extra difficult. You want to be the focus of attention when you are speaking. So ask your audience to ensure speaker view is on. That way when you are speaking, you will in the big video box on your audience's screens.

So using speaker view will allow you to see who is currently speaking and will ensure your face will be prominent when you are speaking to your audience.

A second tip for speaking virtually is to ensure your background matches your message.

ENSURE YOUR BACKGROUND MATCHES YOUR MESSAGE

By now, you probably know that Zoom allows you to use virtual backgrounds. Any image can be a background. A word to the wise: if you want to use a virtual background, ensure the background matches the message you are trying to convey to your audience.

Resist the urge to have what I call a "cutesy" background. Your audience is on the virtual video call to learn something, not to marvel at your background. So don't have pictures of your dog, cat, or child in the background. It will just detract from your message.

Just as a virtual background should match your message, an actual real-life background should also match your message.

If you are giving a class on how to unclutter your house, ensure you have no clutter in your actual background.

If you are giving a class on auto mechanics, why not do it from an auto mechanics shop?

If you are giving a motivational speech, have a motivational background like someone winning a track meet race or someone winning an award or someone walking with artificial legs.

Again, the important thing is that your background supports your message and does not detract from it.

So you now know speaker view will allow you to see who is currently speaking and will ensure your face will be prominent when you are speaking to your audience. You also know it is best to ensure your background matches your message.

But if this third tip is not followed, your virtual experience could be at the very least annoying and, if you are a business owner, if you don't have this, it could make your clients angry and can actually cost you business: stable, high-speed Internet.

USE STABLE, HIGH-SPEED INTERNET

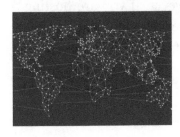 Someone in the audience is talking, and all of a sudden, his or her video freezes. Or someone's voice becomes crackly or even unintelligible. What causes this? There are two main reasons, and they both have to do with the Internet. Reason one is the virtual meeting is being held

at a time of high Internet usage. Reason two is the Internet connection the person is using does not have enough speed to keep up.

We can't do much about the first reason. Even with high-speed Internet, we have no control over Internet usage.

However, we can do something about the second reason: Internet connection speed.

If you are in a rural area, you really just have two choices for Internet: Direct Subscriber Line (DSL) from your phone company or satellite Internet. The reason rural areas don't have cable Internet is the cable company has determined it is not cost effective to put in cable to your property. All you can do is get the fastest speed you can get with DSL or satellite Internet.

If you are in a populated area, you have the choice of going with cable Internet, which has much higher speed than either DSL or satellite Internet.

Your cable company has various plans for Internet speed. My best advice is to get the plan with the highest Internet speed you can afford. If your business is on the Internet—Whose business isn't these days?—I would make an investment in your business by getting the highest Internet speed possible and just pay the cost. If you are on virtual video calls a lot, the extra cost will be well worth it.

Let's talk briefly about Wi-Fi in your home. If you are just attending virtual video calls and are not the host of the meeting, Wi-Fi is probably okay to use. However, if you are hosting a meeting, it is better to connect an Ethernet cable from your cable modem to your computer. The reason for this is Wi-Fi has a slower speed than having an Ethernet line connected to your computer.

***

So the three additional tips for speaking in the virtual world are (1) use speaker view to see who is currently speaking and to ensure your face will be prominent when you are speaking to your audience, (2) ensure your background matches your message, and (3) ensure you have high-speed Internet.

We are not only in the actual world anymore, Toto (*Wizard of Oz* reference). We are also in the Virtual World. Those that understand and exploit it will succeed. Those that don't will not succeed!

CALL TO ACTION

- The next time you use a virtual video communication platform, use speaker view to determine who is speaking.
- The next time you use a virtual video communication platform, ensure your virtual background matches your message.
- Get high-speed Internet.

"Humans are completely incapable of reading and comprehending text on a screen and listening to a speaker at the same time. Therefore, lots of text (almost any text!), and long, complete sentences are bad, Bad, BAD."

—Garr Reynolds

PART VI: PRESENTATION TIPS FOR SPECIFIC SPEAKING SITUATIONS

ALTHOUGH ALL SPEAKING SITUATIONS have much in common, there is specific speaking guidance for different speaking situations. For those who want to become great in a specific speaking situation, this guidance is essential.

The guidance for these different speaking situations takes the form of checklists for before, during, and after the event.

Part VI covers guidance for the following speaking situations:

- Delivering a Keynote Presentation
- Chairing a Meeting
- Facilitating a Meeting
- Serving as Master of Ceremonies
- Presenting Training (Face-to-Face and Online)

DELIVERING A KEYNOTE PRESENTATION

DELIVERING A PRESENTATION IS probably the most familiar speaking situation to most people. Since the majority of this book is dedicated to how to prepare and deliver a great presentation, I will not repeat information here that has already been covered.

However, I will encourage the reader to pay particular attention to this speaking situation because you will be asked to be a speaker one, ten, or many more times in your career. Your ability to stand in front of an audience, string more than two or three words together intelligently, and have a purpose in doing it is the one skill that will propel your career the fastest.

Below are checklists for before, during, and after for times when you volunteered or are required to deliver a presentation:

- Before:
    - Ensure you know everything you possibly can about your audience.
        - Meet with the meeting planner to ask questions about the audience and venue.
    - Tailor your presentation to the audience.
    - If applicable, plan and create slides.
    - Cover only three main points with supporting material for the specific time allowed.
    - Plan to give your audience a call to action with specific tasks for them to accomplish.
    - Plan exactly what you want your audience to know after the presentation; include only this information in your speech and no more.
    - Plan specific gestures, pauses, and movement at specific times during your speech.
    - Plan stories into your speech to emphasize each of the three main points.
    - Plan a specific speech pattern into your speech.
    - Create an introduction that will establish your credibility with your audience.
    - Create an evaluation/marketing form for your audience.
    - Practice, Practice, Practice.

- During:
    - Walk confidently to the lectern.
    - Before your first words, take a deep breath, survey the audience, and then speak.
    - Hand out presentation evaluation form at the beginning of the presentation.
    - Use meaningful gestures to emphasize your three main points.

- Don't apologize for something going wrong in your speech; your audience will not notice it.
- Speak with an air of confidence.
- Don't rush through your speech; your practice will tell you the right rhythm.
- Use varying speeds of speech.
- Vary the pitch of your voice to emphasize your main/ supporting points.

- After:
  - Talk to the event planner to see how he/she thinks your presentation went.
  - Ask the meeting planner for an e-mail list of attendees.
  - Send a message to all attendees with a free PDF report asking them if they want to be put on your newsletter list.

CHAIRING A MEETING

CHANCES ARE SOMETIME IN your career you will be asked to perform as the chair of a meeting. I am sure you have been in other meetings where the performance of the chair was less than it could be. This section will give you guidance on being the chair of a successful meeting.

 A first step to ensure the meeting of which you are the chair is successful is to make sure members understand what the meeting is about and what is expected of them at the meeting. Ensure members know the following when they come to the meeting: (1) the purpose of the meeting, (2) the meeting agenda, (3) the meeting length, and (4) what agenda topics are purely for information purposes and what agenda topics are for discussion.

The majority of the following meeting checklists are from "Chairing a Meeting" (https://www.resourcecentre.org.uk/information/chairing-a-meeting/). Outline your duties as the chair of the meeting before, during, and after the meeting:

- Before:
  - Always ask yourself if a meeting is warranted.
    - Are there other ways to accomplish business outside the meeting or to reduce topics at the meeting?
  - Determine what the desired end result is.
  - Decide whether you need a person to present at the meeting; if so,
    - Give the person enough advance time to prepare the presentation.
    - Allot enough time in the meeting for the presentation.
    - Review the presentation a day ahead of the meeting; have the presenter adjust the presentation as needed.
  - Create and distribute a meeting agenda to all attendees before the meeting encompassing the following:
    - Meeting purpose.
    - Meeting length.
    - Status of previous action items (action items always contain title, description, responsible person [not an organization], due date [rarely changed once established]).
    - Updates on previously discussed topics.
    - New Topics (put list of topics in priority order); indicate on agenda which topics are:
      - For discussion.
      - For decision.
      - For information.

- Action items from this meeting (action items always contain title, description, responsible person [not an organization, due date [rarely changed once established]).
- Besides the agenda, distribute any other needed information to meeting attendees.
- Send out draft agenda three days before soliciting topics.
- Create a meeting evaluation/marketing form for audience.

- During:
  - Ensure:
    - All the business is discussed.
    - Everyone's views are heard.
    - Clear decisions are reached.
    - The meeting starts and finishes on time (late comers will get the message).
  - Welcome new meeting attendees.
  - Facilitate the meeting.
    - Ask people to speak "through the chair." This means putting your hand up if you want to speak and waiting for the chair to say it's your turn.
    - Don't interrupt other people.
    - Stick to the item on the agenda.
    - Don't talk amongst yourselves.
    - Respect other people's views: don't groan or pull faces when someone else is speaking. Wait until they've finished and then explain your point of view calmly and politely.
    - Keep contributions short and to the point.
    - Start and finish the meeting on time.

- At the beginning of the meeting, pass out a meeting evaluation for audience to complete during the meeting and hand to you at the end of the meeting.
- Review agenda.
- Always aim to draw a balance between hearing everyone's views and getting through the business.
- Never use your position as chair as an opportunity to put forward your views to the exclusion of others or to dominate the meeting.
- Let everyone else in the meeting speak first concerning a topic and then offer your opinion.

- After:
  - Allow time after the meeting has finished to talk to new people or follow up suggestions and contributions people made.
  - Talk to your committee members about how the meeting went.
  - Start thinking about the next meeting!

FACILITATING A MEETING

FACILITATING A MEETING IS very different from the other speaking situations. When you are facilitating a meeting, you are ensuring the group meets the objectives of the meeting.

Facilitators should always be outside the group and, preferably, completely outside the organization. The reason for this is facilitators inside the organization or from the group have a tendency to contribute like group members, which is not the role of the facilitator.

From "What is a Facilitator and Other Meeting Roles" (www. co2partners.com/what-is-a-facilitator-role-and-responsibilities/) a meeting facilitator's role is to:

- **Keep the Meeting Focused:** When the group or an individual starts to wander away from the agenda, rein them back in.
- Reduce Confusion:
  - Provide a clear and concise agenda in a timely manner.
  - Arrive early to the meeting to answer questions, test equipment, check on refreshments, and provide direction.
  - Make sure that participants understand and adhere to the rules and agenda.
- **Keep the Leader or Others from Dominating:** Seek to obtain as much valuable input as possible (including minority voices) before closing down a discussion. You may invite quiet participants to speak, respectfully ask the current speaker to wrap up, or call for a vote when the group is divided.

Below are checklists for before, during, and after your facilitation:

- Before:
  - Meet with the head person of the organization to determine:
    - What problem the organization is trying to solve.
    - Who the specific people in the meeting are and what their "agendas" are.
    - How a successful meeting is defined.
    - What the deliverables after the meeting are.
    - What the ground rules for meeting member interactions are.
    - Where specific people should be seated.

- Post-meeting reporting requirements.
- Draft group "ground rules," sample:
  - Everyone respects what other group members say.
  - Do not interrupt another group member.
  - Facilitator may have to cut a group member's comments or group discussion short because of time constraints.
- Visit the meeting venue and determine:
  - Optimal seating arrangement (e.g., U-shaped, audience seating, etc.) for maximum results.
  - How proceedings will be recorded (e.g., flipcharts, PowerPoint, etc.).
  - Will a microphone and sound system be needed; if so, does the venue have this?
- Determine how the facilitator should be dressed.
- Plan to give meeting members a call to action with specific SMART (i.e., specific, measurable, attainable, relevant, time-based) tasks for them to accomplish.
- Plan exactly what you want your audience to know after the meeting.
- Create an introduction explaining why the group has gathered, ground rules for group member interactions.
- Create an evaluation/marketing form for audience.
- Visualize a chronological itinerary of the meeting.

- During:
  - Review with group members:
    - Group "ground rules."
    - Group's challenge to solve.
    - Successful meeting definition.
    - Group meeting deliverables.
    - Group member call to action.
    - How group outcomes will be recorded.
  - Ask every group member to introduce themselves: their name, where they work, what they do, how they feel about the topic, and how they can contribute positively.
  - Continually summarize the discussion.
  - Keep group members on subject.
  - Summarize takeaways from each discussion.

- After:
  - Meeting minutes, record:
    - Attendance.
    - Summaries of discussions.
    - Major decisions.
    - Group/individual group member actions with action description, responsible party, deadline date.
    - Post-meeting.

SERVING AS MASTER OF CEREMONIES

AFTER DELIVERING A PRESENTATION, chairing a meeting, and facilitating a meeting, the next most likely speaking situation is when you are asked to be the Master of Ceremonies (emcee) at an event.

The emcee function can be viewed as the same function a traffic cop performs when electricity is out and he or she is directing traffic because the traffic lights are out. The emcee ensures the event schedule is maintained, introduces the speakers, and generally is responsible for everything at the event going smoothly.

Below are checklists for the emcee for before, during, and after the event. The information came from "What are the Duties of an Emcee?" (https://work.chron.com/duties-emcee-21402.html) and "When You are the Emcee" (https://www.toastmasters.org/magazine/articles/when-you-are-the-emcee).

- Before:
  - Ensure a final agenda is produced.
  - Meet with the event planner to become totally familiar with the audience.
  - Confirm your role with the meeting organizer and be clear about your responsibilities and the organizer's expectations.
  - Research the exact titles for anyone you need to introduce.
  - If your job is to prepare speakers:
    - Find out everything you can about the event well in advance.
    - Tell the speakers the theme, the audience size and background, and the expectations about the content and time limits of their remarks.
    - Tell and preferably show the speakers the logistics, including:
      - Stage setup.
      - Microphone options.
      - Dress code.
      - Keep speakers informed of any changes that may occur.
    - If possible, request a copy of the speakers' remarks or outlines a few days before the event.
      - Reference their remarks in your own comments and review the amount of time each one plans to speak.

- Well in advance of the event, find out each speaker's name—including:
  - Whether they use a middle initial or a hyphenated surname.
  - Learn the correct pronunciation.
  - Write the speakers' names out phonetically and practice it out loud so you can say it with ease and demonstrate your respect for the person.
- Perform an on-site rehearsal well in advance of the event:
  - Sound check.
  - Lighting check.
  - Become familiar with the stage space and lectern.
  - Microphone: lectern only, lap mike, microphone with a cord.
- Introduce yourself to the speakers either in person or on the phone before the event.

- During:
  - Your energy, confidence, and sincerity should match the spirit of the event.
  - Never leave the stage empty; wait for the speaker at the lectern, shake his/her hand, and then leave to the designated spot for you to wait until the speaker is finished.
  - As the first person that the audience sees, the emcee represents the sponsoring organization to the audience members.
    - Set down some rules of the house and dispense any additional information as needed.
      - Point out the location of the emergency exits and the restrooms.

- If food is served, the emcee lets the audience know when they can and can't order.
- Carefully keep track of time that any opening speakers take while on stage so that the headliner speaker is assured of his/her full time slot.
- If a speaker starts to run long or over time, the emcee signals to someone in the house, who flashes a light on the performer.
  - This tells the speaker to finish up and get off stage or that they have a specified amount of time, for example, five minutes, to finish his act and get off the stage.
  - In between the changing of the speakers, it's also important for the emcee to keep the level of the crowd up and excited.
- After the last speaker has ended and left the stage, the emcee reappears to thank the speakers and the crowd.
- Prepare yourself for the unexpected (e.g., fire alarm sounds, a speaker forgets her notes, a technology glitch occurs, etc.).
- Emcee thanks the audience.
  - Reminds the audience of any other upcoming events and informs them about other ways to keep up with information from the sponsoring organization, for example:
    - Signing up for the newsletter.
    - Subscribing to an email list.
    - Following the sponsoring organization on social media.

- After:
  - Ask for feedback from the meeting organizer, other speakers, and audience members.
    - Review the video, if there is one.
    - Ask what worked well and what could work better next time.
    - Ask a colleague in the audience to time each segment so you can compare the actual timing against the original plan.
      - Ask for the colleague's timing notes.
  - The information you gather can help you prepare for the next event you emcee.
  - Be sure to follow up and thank all the speakers and everyone who helped make the event a success.

PRESENTING TRAINING (FACE-TO-FACE AND ONLINE)

CHANCES ARE SOMETIME IN your career you will be asked to train someone to do something. Poof! You are a trainer. You may also be asked to develop the training slides. You will quickly find out the first time that to teach a subject you must be two to three levels of understanding below the level of understanding of your students.

There are many common tasks to accomplish for both face-to-face and online training. However, there are additional online training only tasks.

Below are checklists for before, during, and after your training divided by tasks common to face-to-face and online training and online training only:

- Before:
  - Both Face-to-Face and Online:
    - Ensure you know everything you possibly can about your audience.
    - Plan and create slides.
    - Plan to give your audience a call to action with specific tasks for them to accomplish.
    - Plan exactly what you want your audience to know after the presentation; include only this information in your speech and no more.
    - Plan specific gestures, pauses, and movement at specific times during your training.
    - Plan stories into your training to emphasize your main points.
    - Create an introduction that will establish your credibility with your audience.
    - Create a facilitation evaluation/marketing form for audience.
    - Create an evaluation/marketing form for audience.
    - Practice, Practice, Practice.
  - Online Only:
    - Select the online training system to use.
    - Become proficient in online training system.
    - Secure the services of a moderator who will actually run the online training; you are the teacher, not the moderator.
    - Clarify features you as the speaker and the moderator will be able to access.

- Decide:
  - How long your online training will be.
  - How many participants will be in the training.
  - Whether you want to use a webinar format (50+ participants, little interaction with participants) or more interactive training (< 50 participants, chat room).

- During:
  - Both Face-to-Face and Online:
    - Introduce yourself and your program.
    - How long the program is.
    - Breaks.
    - Question and answer policy.
    - Give your audience a call to action with specific tasks for them to accomplish.
    - Use specific gestures, pauses, and movement at specific times during your training.
    - Use stories to your training to emphasize your main points.
    - Plan a change in your presentation every fifteen minutes, for example:
      - Show a video.
      - Ask your audience questions.
      - Hold an exercise.
      - Pass around a prop.
      - Tell a relevant story.
    - Summarize everything you have gone over so far after each segment of your training. Repetition helps participants remember your presentation points.
  - Face-to-Face Training Only:

- Explain where restrooms are.
- Other items for in-person meetings.
- Online Training Only:
  - Review what online features participants, speaker, moderator can access.
  - Moderator:
    - Interpose speaker and speaker's slides.
    - Summarize chat questions/comments and present them to speaker.

- After:
  - Ask attendees to hand in or e-mail the evaluation/ marketing form to you.
  - Talk to the meeting planner to see how he/she thinks your presentation went.
  - Ask the meeting planner for an e-mail list of attendees.
  - Send a message to all attendees with a free PDF report asking them if they want to be put on your newsletter list.

FINAL THOUGHTS

I HAVE TAKEN YOU on a journey in this book. A journey where you examine the quality of your speaking and determine whether this quality is where you want it to be or whether it needs to be improved substantially.

Remember when you were a small child. If you saw something that was disagreeable to you, whether it was a scary movie, your mother scolding you, or a teacher unhappy with you, you just covered your eyes and then the bad thing would go away, right? Wrong! If your speaking is not up to where you want it to be, you can't just figuratively close your eyes and make it go away. It won't!

Remember, there are two challenges you face in becoming a great speaker. The first challenge is realizing improving your skills will advance your life and career. The second challenge is putting in the time to study and practice, emphasis on practice, to really improve your presentation skills.

In the introduction of this book, I said the first challenge is much harder to overcome than the second. You have to take the first step; you have to open yourself up to admitting to yourself and others that you need to improve your speaking ability; you have to face your fear of speaking and drive right through it to victory.

Michelangelo said, "The greater danger for most of us lies not in setting our aim too high and falling short; but in setting our aim too low and achieving our mark."

Set your aim high and strive to become the best speaker you can be. Even if you fall short, the journey you take in striving to be a better speaker will make you a better speaker today than you were yesterday and a better speaker tomorrow than you are today. Improving your speaking is incremental. It takes a lot of practice, as does anything else worth doing.

Improving your presentation skills will have an immediate effect on your career and your life the minute you start improving your presentation skills and proving it to yourself in front of an audience. There is nothing quite like the spectacular feeling you get when you have "hit a home run" in giving a speech to an applauding audience.

As I have mentioned previously, as a Toastmaster for over thirty years and in my business, I have seen miraculous improvements in self-confidence in people striving to be the best speaker they can be. A funny thing happens on the way to becoming the best speaker you can be. Your self-confidence in other areas of your life increases and your quality of life goes up.

Remember what Earl Nightingale said: "Luck is when preparedness meets opportunity." Opportunities will always come your way. The only questions is will you be prepared?

In the introduction, I told you I wrote this book for the person who wants to be a passable speaker, the person who wants to speak for a living, and the person who wants to become a "concert pianist" of speaking.

Why not strive to be the "concert pianist" of speaking? If you do, you will open your life to more happiness than you can imagine.

It all starts with YOU TAKING ACTION!!!

RESOURCES

Anderson, Chris. *TED Talks: The Official TED Guide to Public Speaking*. Houghton, Mifflin, Harcourt, 2016. Print, eBook

Carnegie, Dale. *The Art of Public Speaking*. New York, NY: Fall River Press, 1915. Print, eBook

Carnegie, Dale. *Public Speaking for Success*. New York, NY: Penguin Group, 2005 (revised from the original 1926 book by Dale Carnegie). Print, eBook

Gallo, Carmine. *The Presentation Secrets of Steve Jobs: How to Be Insanely Great in Front of Any Audience*. New York, NY: McGraw-Hill, 2010. Print, eBook

Handley, Ann. *Everybody Writes: Your Go-To Guide to Creating Ridiculously Good Content*. Hoboken, New Jersey: Wiley, 2014. Print, eBook

Leeds, Dorothy. *PowerSpeak: The Complete Guide to Successful Persuasion.* New York, NY: Berkley Books, 1988. Print, eBook

Maxey, Cyndi & O'Connor, Kevin. *Present Like a Pro: The Field Guide to Mastering the Art of Business, Professional, and Public Speaking.* New York, NY: St. Martin's Griffin, 2006. Print, eBook

Sanow, Arnold J. & Lescault, Henry J., *Present with Power, Punch, and Pizzazz: The Ultimate Guide to Delivering Presentations with Poise, Persuasion, and Professionalism.* Bloomington, IN: iUniverse, Inc., 2011. Print, eBook

Shapira, Allison, *Speak with Impact: How to Command the Room and Influence Others.* New York, NY: Harper Collins Leadership, 2018. Print, eBook

Walters, Lilly. *Secrets of Successful Speakers: Wisdom from the Greatest Motivators of Our Time.* New York, NY: McGraw-Hill, 1993. Print

Walters, Lilly. *Secrets of Superstar Speakers: How You Can Motivate, Captivate & Persuade.* New York, NY: McGraw-Hill, 2000. Print

ABOUT THE AUTHOR

FRANK DIBARTOLOMEO IS A retired U.S. Air Force Lieutenant Colonel. His expertise as an engineer and technical leader has led to a variety of leadership assignments as a practicing program manager and systems engineer, including assignments at the Air Force Research Laboratory, the Pentagon and, as a contractor, the Deputy Lead Engineer on a three hundred–person national security program.

Frank is also an award-winning speaker, public speaking coach, and seminar leader. He has developed and honed his extensive public speaking abilities over his forty-year career, both in military service and as a contractor. Frank has significantly influenced military, U.S. government, and industry leaders in their decisions of national security importance.

Because of his outstanding work in the field of public speaking and leadership, in 2002, Frank was awarded Toastmasters

International's highest individual award: Distinguished Toastmaster.

He formed DiBartolomeo Consulting International (DCI), LLC in 2007. The mission of DCI is to help program managers, scientists, and engineers to inspire, motivate, and influence their colleagues and other technical professionals through improving their presentation skills, communication, and personal presence.

Frank can be reached at frank@speakleadandsucceed.com.

ACKNOWLEDGMENTS

I THINK EVERYONE THINKS of writing a book at one time or another in their life. I am no exception. In a way, this has been a long journey since I joined Toastmasters more than thirty years ago with many people along the way helping me.

I first thank my speaking business coach, Arnold Sanow, CSP (Ceritified Speaking Professional) for his guidance, wisdom, and never-ending positive attitude. He was and still is my "scout" and "guide" as we travel the "jungles" of the speaking business world.

I thank my fellow Toastmasters from the Wright Flyers (Wright-Patterson AFB OH), the Burke Toastmasters (Burke, VA), the TASC Toastmasters (Chantilly), and the Toast of Tysons Toastmasters (Tysons Corner, VA). You all had a part in my writing this book on public speaking.

I thank all my fellow National Speakers Association (NSA) Washington DC Chapter members. You have been an inspiration to me. This book would literally have not been possible without your advice, encouragement, and belief in me!

I thank all my friends for encouraging me to write this book. It really has been a labor of love.

I thank all of you for adding to my public speaking "quiver" the necessary "arrows" that provided the content for this book.

DCI

DiBartolomeo Consulting International (DCI), LLC

6183 Snowhill Court
Centerville, Virginia 20120
Office – (703) 815-1324
Cell – (703) 509-4424
www.speakleadandsucceed.com
info@speakleadandsucceed.com

*Helping Technical Professionals to Improve Their
Presentation Skills, Communication, and Personal Presence!*

As the **_purchaser_** of this book, you are entitled to a no obligation, **_one hour, one-on-one conversation with Frank DiBartolomeo_** to answer your presentation skills questions and challenges. Please send an e-mail to frank@speakleadandsucceed. com and **_he will get back to you within twenty-four hours._**

In addition, every person who meets with Frank will receive a FREE subscription to DCI's weekly newsletter and also gets a FREE PDF Electronic Copy of the following packet of DCI reports: (1) How to Use Your Listening Skills to Become a Better Speaker, (2) How to Use Gestures to Greatly Enhance Your Presentations,

(3) How to Deftly Field Audience Questions, (4) How to Dress for Success When Speaking, (5) What to Do When Things Go Wrong in Your Presentation.

If you need assistance with presentation skills or interview skills, please send an e-mail for no obligation to info@speakleadandsucceed.com or reply to the information inquiry form at www.speakleadandsucceed.com.

If you are interested in using Frank's services in any of the following areas, please feel free to contact Frank anytime:

- Improving Your Presentation Skills
- Conquering Your Fear of Speaking
- 3 Ways Public Speaking Adds to Your Power
- Injecting Stories into Your Speaking
- How to Prepare for an Interview

CPSIA information can be obtained
at www.ICGtesting.com
Printed in the USA
LVHW030600220121
677170LV00003B/89

9 781646 632404